T0193997

Creating a Life I Love

A Practical Study Guide for Overcoming Unwanted
Habits and Adopting Desirable Ones

Tim Bradley, MA, LMFT

CREATING A LIFE I LOVE
A PRACTICAL STUDY GUIDE FOR OVERCOMING UNWANTED HABITS AND ADOPTING DESIRABLE ONES

Copyright © 2015 Tim Bradley, MA, LMFT.

All rights reserved. No part of this book may be used or reproduced by any means, graphic, electronic, or mechanical, including photocopying, recording, taping or by any information storage retrieval system without the written permission of the author except in the case of brief quotations embodied in critical articles and reviews.

iUniverse books may be ordered through booksellers or by contacting:

iUniverse
1663 Liberty Drive
Bloomington, IN 47403
www.iuniverse.com
1-800-Authors (1-800-288-4677)

Because of the dynamic nature of the Internet, any web addresses or links contained in this book may have changed since publication and may no longer be valid. The views expressed in this work are solely those of the author and do not necessarily reflect the views of the publisher, and the publisher hereby disclaims any responsibility for them.

Any people depicted in stock imagery provided by Thinkstock are models, and such images are being used for illustrative purposes only.
Certain stock imagery © Thinkstock.

ISBN: 978-1-4917-7241-6 (sc)
ISBN: 978-1-49177-243-0 (e)

Library of Congress Control Number: 2015911124

Print information available on the last page.

iUniverse rev. date: 9/24/2014

Creating a Life I Love: Study Guide
Table of Contents

Creating a Life I Love: Study Guide
Table of Contents

CONTENTS

ORIENTATION *(vertical side text)*

Strategy: **Orientation to Training**

Congratulations and welcome to *Creating a Life I Love* basic training! You have endured countless obstacles in life, and you are still breathing. You are a survivor. Now that the hardest part is out of the way, you can focus on what it takes to not just endure life but to create it on purpose, no matter what obstacles you face. In this training you will learn about, strengthen, and begin to master effective, evidence-based strategies designed to help you restructure your thoughts, regulate your emotions, and reinforce your behaviors in ways that powerfully inspire and move you to create a life you love. The material in this guide works best when used with a personal coach. However, depending on your level of commitment, you can learn and practice these strategies and skills all on your own. However you take this journey, I congratulate you for taking action to create a life you love!

Purpose: Receive an overview of how *Creating A Life I Love* basic training will train your brain and body to create and live a life you love.

Acquire: **Training Topics**

Focus on changing to ensure more of the same. Focus on creating, and anything is possible.

- neuroplasticity— reprogramming your brain
- four stages of habit development
- basic training map

- evidence-based training
- training assumptions
- basic training schedule
- basic training options
- training targets

Training Objectives

1. Describe three states of mind and the skill sets to master each.
2. Describe the purpose of assumptions used in this training.
3. Describe three of your favorite training assumptions used in this training.
4. Describe three pretraining and three training targets.
5. Determine your commitment to training and practice.

Strengthen: **Practice Exercises**

- Identify the pros and cons for committing to training and practice.
- Determine your commitment to training and practice.

Generalize: **Home Fun**

- Be mindful of the commitment you have made to create a life you love.
- Make a list of anything that may interfere with keeping your commitment.
- For each potential interference, create a counterinterference that will ensure that you keep your commitment.

Neuroplasticity—Reprogramming Your Brain

The human brain is composed of approximately one hundred billion neurons. Early researchers believed that neurogenesis, or the creation of new neurons, stopped shortly after birth. Today, it is understood that the brain possesses the remarkable capacity to reorganize pathways, create new connections, and alter existing ones in order to adapt to new experiences, learn new information, and create new memories. Neurons that are used frequently develop stronger connections, and those that are rarely or never used eventually die. By developing new connections and pruning away weak ones, the brain is able to adapt to a changing environment. *Brain plasticity*, also known as neuroplasticity or cortical remapping, is a term that refers to the brain's ability to change and adapt as a result of experience. *Functional plasticity* refers to the brain's ability to move functions from a damaged area of the brain to other undamaged areas. *Structural plasticity* refers to the brain's ability to actually change its physical structure as a result of learning.

Your habits are nothing more than strong neural pathways of thought, emotion, and behavior. The more you think, feel, and act in a consistent way, the stronger those neural pathways become. Your brain is wired to follow the strongest pathways when processing information. This is why it seems so difficult to break an unwanted habit and start a new one. By participating in this training, your brain will literally begin to create new neural pathways of thinking, feeling, and behaving. The more you practice the strategies and skills presented in this study guide, the stronger those new pathways will become and the more your old unwanted pathways will shrink and fade away due to lack of use.

Four Stages of Habit Development

Habits are developed in four stages: orientation, acquisition, strengthening, and generalization. In the orientation stage you observe the new behavior and begin to become familiar with the language attached to it. At the end of the orientation stage you are able to briefly describe the language and behavior you are attempting to habituate. In the acquisition stage you break the new behavior down into smaller behaviors or skills, and you learn specific strategies to help master those skills. At the end of the acquisition stage you are able to verbally describe the strategies and skills necessary to create the new behavior. In the strengthening stage you refine and strengthen the strategies and skills through consistent repetition and practice. At the end of the strengthening stage you are able to describe and demonstrate the desired behavior. You have reached the generalization stage when you find yourself using the new language and acting out the new behaviors automatically without thinking.

Each chapter of this study guide is divided into four sections that correspond with the four stages of habit development. The *orientation* section is the first page of each chapter. It includes a general description of the chapter, the purpose of the chapter, a list of topics that will be discussed, training objectives, practice exercises, and home fun (homework). Strategies and skills are described in the *acquisition* section. Practice exercises are provided in the *strengthening* section, and home fun assignments are provided in the *generalization* section.

ACQUISITION

Creating a Life I Love: Study Guide
Session 1: Orientation to Training

Creating a Life I Love Basic Training Map

The following training map is designed to help you visualize the cognitive, emotional, and behavioral systems of your brain. The cognitive system is referred to as *reason mind*. The emotional system is referred to as *emotion mind*, and the behavioral system is referred to simply as *behavior*. The information below the map briefly describes each system and the corresponding concepts, strategies, and skills that help produce new ways of thinking, responding to emotions, and behaving.

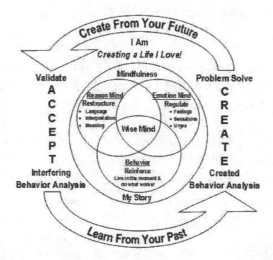

System	Strategy/Skill
Cognitive-emotional-behavioral system. The quality of your life is based upon how you respond to your thoughts, emotions, and behaviors. Each system interacts with the others to produce a way of being in the world.	Mindfulness. Mindfulness is a simple set of skills that helps you observe what is going on in the moment inside and outside of you without judgment so that you have access to your own wisdom to think, feel, and do what works.
Reason mind. The reason mind is the areas of your brain that produce language, interpretations, meaning, and your story about life. Nothing means anything until your reason mind makes it so.	Restructure thoughts. These strategies empower you to choose styles and constructs of thinking that evoke desired emotional energies and move you to create a life you love.
Emotion mind. The emotion mind is the areas of your brain that produce feelings, sensations, and urges. Your emotion mind produces energies that move you.	Regulate emotions. These skills empower you to create more positive emotions, decrease your vulnerability to negative emotions, help move you from one emotional state to another, and increase positive emotional states.
Wise mind. Wisdom comes from observing and describing your thoughts, emotions, behaviors, and environment without judgment and doing what works in the moment.	Reinforce behavior. These if-then techniques can effectively decrease or eliminate your interfering behavior and turn your desired way of being into habit.

ACQUISITION

Creating a Life I Love: Study Guide
Session 1: Orientation to Training

ACQUISITION

Accept

- **Accept what you know is just a story.** Your story is a summation of all your interpretations of your perceptions of your life experiences. Your story rarely reflects what actually happened or what is happening in life because all you are able to do is perceive and interpret.

- **Accept what happened in your past.** You cannot change your past. What happened has happened. Focusing on changing it ensures more of the same.

- **Accept what is in the moment.** Accept what is before you. You are the way you are. Others are the way they are, and the world is the way it is.

- **Practice validation and radical acceptance.** This strategy encourages acceptance and trust of self, others, and the world.

- **Do an interfering-behavior analysis.** This mindfulness exercise helps you to observe and describe without judgment behavior that interferes with living a life you love.

- **I am.** Consider the possibility that who you believed yourself to be earlier in life was learned primarily from your caregivers. It makes sense that you believed them, but when you take responsibility for what you value in life, how and what you think, and how you respond to your emotions, urges, those around you, and your environment, you take charge of who you are.

Create

- **Create your story.** Most of your past story was created without your awareness. However, you can choose to become the conscious author of your current and future story. As the sole author, you can create a story that powerfully moves and inspires you to live a life you love.

- **Learn from your past.** The process of discovering what doesn't work is critical to creating something new that does.

- **Create from your future.** Focus your mind on possibilities from your future that move and inspire you. Then take action right now to make them a reality.

- **Problem solve.** Utilize strategies and skills that create different ways of thinking, feeling, and behaving.

- **Do a created-behavior analysis.** This exercise helps you to create a desired way of being and matching behaviors that with practice become automatic.

- **Create your way of being.** You may choose to be the same as your past or create a completely different way of being. Creating a way of being requires learning and practicing simple sets of skills. With commitment, practice, and perseverance, old, ineffective habits of thinking, behaving, and feeling can be replaced by ones that match your created way of being.

Accept that there is no substitute for consistent observation, commitment, practice, and perseverance when creating a life you love. A good coach will push you beyond what you think you are capable of and help you realize goals you never thought you could achieve. If you wish to excel quickly and efficiently, it pays to have a coach and to be coachable.

Creating a Life I Love: Study Guide
Session 1: Orientation to Training

Evidence-Based Training

Creating A Life I Love basic training teaches a blend of effective strategies and skills that are based upon the best available research and drawn from the therapeutic models listed below. You can read the research and learn more about these theories and methods by referring to the Further Reading section at the end of this book.

Therapeutic Models

Dialectical behavior therapy (DBT) is a cognitive-behavioral therapeutic approach developed by psychologist Dr. Marsha Linehan for the treatment of chronically suicidal and self-injurious individuals with borderline personality disorder (BPD). DBT balances problem-solving strategies and acceptance strategies with an emphasis on dialectical processes. DBT is recommended by the National Registry of Evidence-based Programs and Practices for psychosocial adjustment, cooccurring disorders, and mental health inpatient and outpatient treatment. It is one of the most effective evidence-based treatments for depression and suicide prevention.

Narrative therapy is a postmodern therapeutic approach that explores a person's stories about life and how interpretations of life experiences serve to reinforce fixed ways of being. Cognitive restructuring strategies are used to intentionally create life stories that free us from the constraints of rigid interpretations and inspire us to create and live lives we love.

Positive psychology is founded on the belief that people want to lead meaningful and fulfilling lives, cultivate what is best within them, and enhance their experiences of love, work, and play. Positive psychology has three central concerns: positive emotions, positive individual traits, and positive institutions. Understanding positive emotions entails the study of contentment with the past, happiness in the present, and hope for the future. Understanding positive individual traits consists of the study of the strengths and virtues, such as the capacity for love, work, courage, compassion, resilience, creativity, curiosity, integrity, self-knowledge, moderation, self-control, and wisdom. Understanding positive institutions entails the study of the strengths that foster better communities, such as justice, responsibility, civility, parenting, nurturance, work ethic, leadership, teamwork, purpose, and tolerance.

Outcomes

- decreased suicide attempts
- decreased self-injurious behaviors
- increased psychosocial adjustment
- increased training retention
- decreased symptoms of eating disorders
- decreased drug use

- increased quality of relationships
- increased confidence in conducting life
- increased personal productivity
- increased joy

- families and schools that allow children to flourish
- workplaces that foster satisfaction and high productivity
- communities that encourage civic engagement
- therapists who identify and nurture their patients' strengths
- the teaching of positive psychology
- dissemination of positive psychology interventions in organizations and communities

ACQUISITION

Training Assumptions

The following assumptions are not true or false, right or wrong. Although opposite assumptions are equally valid, these are constructed to intentionally increase your emotional positivity.

- **People need to feel safe and significant.** Our personal well-being is enhanced when we feel safe and significant.

- **Dignity and respect are basic human needs that are given freely and not earned.** The best way to create respect is to genuinely express it to ourselves and others.

- **People are perfect, whole, and complete. There is nothing wrong.** There never has been, and there never will be. No matter how much we change, we can never be anyone other than ourselves—no more, no less: perfect, whole, and complete.

- **People are doing the best they can.** Based upon our unique genetic makeup, life development, experiences, and environment, it makes perfect sense that we do what we do. "Shoulding" on self or others is rarely effective.

- **People want to improve.** We generally want the best out of life even if we do not know how to get it.

- **Pain and stress are inevitable parts of life.** Accepting pain and stress as inevitable parts of life relieves us from emotional suffering.

- **Although people may not have caused all their problems, it is up to them to accept them and/or solve them.** To blame anyone or anything is futile. It is ultimately up to us to take full responsibility for our own thoughts, feelings, and actions.

- **The present moment is all that exists.** Your past and future do not exist in the present and never have. Right now is the only time and place you can learn from your past, create from your future, and do what works.

- **People can create new ways of being.** We do not have to be slaves to our past. We have the option, if we choose, to create our present reality out of possibilities from our future and create a way of being that we love.

- **Thoughts are nothing from which everything is created.** All I know is that I know nothing. It is from nothing that everything is created.

- **Emotions can be regulated.** Harness the energy of your emotions and you can be at peace, in love, and full of joy—even if you live in hell.

- **People can create new habits in all relative contexts.** Any behavior performed and rewarded often enough can become automatic. The most effective way to change an old habit is to create a new one to take its place.

- **Creating new behaviors requires commitment, repetition, and perseverance.** There is no substitute for commitment, repetition, and perseverance in order to achieve mastery.

- **People cannot fail.** If something didn't work, we have simply not found the way to make it happen.

- **People need support.** Effectively supporting each other involves capitalizing on each other's strengths and compensating for each other's weaknesses.

ACQUISITION

Creating a Life I Love Basic Training Schedule

ACQUISITION

Session One

Orientation. Receive an overview of how *Creating A Life I Love* basic training will train your brain and body to create and live a life you love!

Session Two

Mindfulness. Develop a lifestyle of participation with awareness that empowers you to gain access to your own intuitive inner wisdom to do what works in the moment.

Session Three

Interfering- and Created-Behavior Analyses. Discover when, where, and how specific behaviors interfere with living a life you love. Create a way of being that powerfully inspires and moves you. Then develop a script to restructure your thoughts, regulate your emotions, and reinforce behaviors that match your created way of being. Practice and adjust your script until your desired behaviors become automatic.

Session Four

Restructure Thoughts. Choose styles of thinking, empowering thoughts, and assumptions that move you to act on your created way of being.

Session Five

Regulate Emotions. Learn to recognize and regulate emotions so they do not regulate you. Increase positive emotions, and decrease your vulnerability to negative ones.

Session Six

Reinforce Behaviors. Learn how to use eight basic methods to effectively decrease or eliminate your interfering behavior and turn your desired way of being into habit.

Session Seven

Radically Accept. Learn the conversation of love that radically accepts yourself, others, and the world without judgment; balances the stress of change; encourages greater trust and openness; strengthens relationships; and moves you to live a life you love.

Session Eight

Respond to Stress. Learn how to tolerate stress, stay in the moment without making it worse, and let go of emotional suffering.

Moving Forward. Celebrate *Creating A Life I Love!*

Basic Training Options

The following training and service options are available through PathWise Productions Inc. You can reach Tim, the founder and CEO of PathWise Productions Inc. at tim@pathwiseproductions.com, or visit pathwiseproductions.com for more information.

Creating A Life I Love Basic Training:
- Eight group sessions are designed to help you quickly learn, strengthen, and begin to master effective, evidence-based strategies that powerfully move you to create and live a life you love.
- Individualized interfering- and created-behavior analyses are designed to help you observe and describe behaviors that interfere with creating a life you love and replace them with habits that match the person you create yourself to be.
- Twenty-four/seven telephone coaching is in place to assist you in meeting your goals.

Basic Training and Individual Coaching:
- You get everything in Basic Training plus four private coaching sessions.

Beyond the Basics
PathWise Parenting Options

PathWise Parenting:
- Eight group sessions are designed to help you quickly learn, strengthen, and begin to master effective, evidence-based strategies that powerfully move you and your family to create lives you love.
- Two caregivers may participate for the price of one.
- Twenty-four/seven telephone coaching is in place to assist you in meeting your goals.

PathWise Parenting and Individual Coaching:
- You get everything in PathWise Parenting plus four private coaching sessions.

You will learn to
- develop an effective style of parenting,
- understand your child's emotional development,
- create empowering character qualities,
- identify interfering behaviors,
- communicate and develop love and self-esteem,
- keep from being trapped in a corner,
- master the secrets of the super nannies, and
- establish meaningful and memorable family moments.

Train your children to
- say yes to creating lives they love,
- get in the moment to do what works,
- regulate their emotions so their emotions don't regulate you and them,
- stay in the moment without making it worse, and
- get what they want while respecting self and others.

8

Creating a Life I Love: Study Guide
Session 1: Orientation to Training

PathWise Mental Health Services

PathWise mental health services utilize effective, evidence-based therapeutic models to treat individuals, children, couples, or families with the following problems:

- **addictions**
- **attention deficit disorder (ADD)**
- **attention deficit hyperactivity disorder (ADHD)**
- **anxiety disorders**
  - general anxiety
  - panic disorders
  - phobias
  - post-traumatic stress disorder (PTSD)
- **mood disorders**
  - bipolar
  - depression
  - seasonal affective disorder
- **schizophrenia**
- **personality disorders**
  - borderline personality disorder (BPD)
- **individual and relationships**
  - individuals
  - children
  - couples
  - families

PathWise to Success

PathWise Productions is committed to helping you succeed in the workplace. Whether you are an employee or an entrepreneur, PathWise is available to help you increase your work satisfaction and productivity, generate and attain your goals, and systematically succeed at creating a work or business experience you love.

Pretraining Targets

1. **Develop a trusting relationship.** *People need to feel safe and significant.* The first pretraining target is to develop a trusting relationship with your trainers and allow them to develop a trusting relationship with you.
2. **Orient to training.** *People are doing the best they can and want to improve.*
   - **Roles**
     o **Coach.** With your permission, your trainers will be your life coaches. Every great player has a great coach. Your coaches can help you achieve more than you might ever be able to achieve all by yourself.
     o **Player.** Your role, if you choose to accept it, will be the player. With the help of your coaches, you can effectively and successfully attain your goals and create a life you love.

   - **Responsibilities**
     o **Coach.** Your coach's job is to teach you how to create more effective ways of being, thinking, feeling, and behaving; provide regular and consistent opportunities to practice these new skills; model the skills so that you can see what they look like; and help you document your progress throughout your training.
     o **Player.** Your job as a player is to learn, practice, and generalize these skills in your life until you are able to use them without thinking when you need them the most.

   - **Reason**
     o To create and live a life you love!

   - **Process**
     o **Strategies and skills training and practice.** You will learn how to create and sustain your own desired way of being, get and stay in the moment to do what works, employ powerful structures of thought, regulate your emotions so they don't regulate you, strengthen effective behaviors and reduce interfering behaviors, tolerate stress and pain, and communicate love and encouragement to yourself and others.
     o **Interfering-behavior analysis.** This process is designed to help you accept that your behaviors make sense and that there is nothing wrong with you. It helps you to identify the triggers, natural desires, and rewards that move you to behave in ways that interfere with living a life you love and helps you to find simple actions that can reduce or eliminate your interfering behaviors. It helps you to discern thoughts, emotions, and behaviors that work in specific settings and those that do not. It is like looking at a clip of a movie you created. You created the story that didn't work, and you can also create a story that does.
     o **Created-behavior analysis and practice.** After you see what happened, what worked, and what didn't work in specific settings, the created-behavior analysis helps you to create your way of being *on purpose*. It helps you to reduce behaviors that do not work and to create new thoughts, emotions, and behaviors that match your created way of being. As with every new way of being and behaving, it becomes easier and more automatic the more you practice what works.

ACQUISITION

3. **Make a commitment.** *Creating new behaviors requires commitment, practice, and perseverance.* Creating a habit of living a life you love depends entirely on your level of commitment to create, practice, and reward behaviors that match your created way of being. You are welcome to be a spectator in the process. However, for your participation in training to be most effective, it is recommended that you make at least a level 2 commitment to being coachable.

> Level 0: "I am not committed to and I do not want to participate in this training."
> Level 1: "I want to do something different and would just like to watch."
> Level 2: "I am willing to work with a coach and be coachable to create a life I love."
> Level 3: "I am in it to win it and will work with or without a coach to create a life I love."

Training Targets

1. **Create consistent training and practice behaviors.** The most effective way to learn new thoughts, feelings, and behaviors is to practice them until they become automatic. If you do not practice new behaviors you might never create a life you love. The first training target is to identify and replace training-interfering thoughts, emotions, and behaviors with those that consistently inspire you to train and practice.

2. **Increase effective strategies and skills.** Throughout your training you will learn, practice, strengthen, and generalize effective strategies and skills that will help you think, behave, and feel in ways that help you create and live a life you love.

3. **Create and live a life you love.** Throughout your life you have naturally learned ways to avoid or react to painful experiences that may work for a while but in the long run make your life more difficult. The third training target is to replace behaviors that interfere with creating and living a life you love with behaviors that match the person you create yourself to be.

ACQUISITION

Practice Exercises

Pros and Cons of Training and Practice

Complete the pros and cons for and against committing to this training by filling in each section below.

Committing to Training and Practice

Pros	Cons

Not Committing to Training and Practice

Pros	Cons

STRENGTHENING

Creating a Life I Love: Study Guide
Session 1: Orientation to Training

Determine Your Commitment to Training and Practice

- ❑ Level 0: "I am not committed to and I do not want to participate in this training."
- ❑ Level 1: "I want to do something different and would just like to watch."
- ❑ Level 2: "I am willing to work with a coach and be coachable to create a life I love."
- ❑ Level 3: "I am in it to win it and will work with or without a coach to create a life I love."

For level 2 commitment or higher:

- ❑ I agree to attend and complete every training session on time as scheduled.
- ❑ I agree to actively participate in every session.
- ❑ I agree to practice the skills I learn throughout the training.
- ❑ I am not able to keep the above agreements and can commit to the following:

_____
_____
_____
_____
_____
_____
_____
_____

- ❑ What I would like to get out of this training:

_____
_____
_____
_____
_____
_____
_____
_____

_____   _____   _____
TRAINEE NAME (PRINT)   SIGNATURE   DATE

STRENGTHENING

Home Fun

GENERALIZATION

- Be mindful of the promise you have made here today throughout the rest of this training period.
- Be mindful of things that may interfere with keeping your commitment, and make arrangements that will increase the probability of maintaining your commitment to training.
- Troubleshooting:
  1. Make a list of anything that may get in the way or interfere with keeping your commitment.
  2. For each potential interference, create a counterinterference that when acted upon will ensure that you keep your commitment.

_____

_____

_____

_____

_____

_____

_____

_____

_____

_____

_____

Creating a Life I Love: Study Guide
Session 2: Mindfulness

Skill: **Mindfulness**

Mindfulness is the process of separating and observing your thoughts, emotions, behaviors, and surroundings, describing them without judgment, and then choosing to do what works in the present moment. It is a special state of being in which you experience calmness, spaciousness, presence, connectedness, and awareness. Mindfulness helps you to participate fully in life from moment to moment, free from the constraints of the past and the self-fulfilling prophesies of the future. It is a way of controlling your mind so that your mind does not control you.

Purpose: Develop a lifestyle of participation with awareness that empowers you to gain access to your own intuitive inner wisdom to do what works in the moment.

Acquire: **Training Topics**
- mastering your mind
- *what* skills
- *how* skills
- reasons to get in the moment

There is no ttime like the present. It is the only pplace you can learn from your past, create from yyour future, and do what works

Training Objectives
1. Describe one reason for learning mindfulness.
2. Describe why your past and future do not exist.
3. Describe what your future will probably look like if you consistently live in the past.
4. Describe three *what* and three *how* skills.
5. Observe and describe the behavior(s) that interfere most with creating and living a life you love.

Strengthen: **Practice Exercises**
- getting mindful of the moment
- identifying interfering behaviors

Generalize: **Home Fun**
- Practice mindfulness throughout the day. Be mindful each time you change an activity, and be mindful of the many different activities you engage in.
- Be mindful of your interfering behaviors and those behaviors that work for you.
- Note what you were mindful of, and note the results of being mindful.

ORIENTATION

Creating a Life I Love: Study Guide
Session 2: Mindfulness

Mastering Your Mind

MINDFULNESS

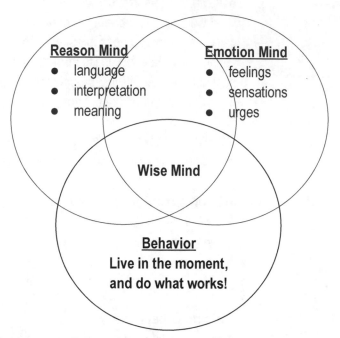

Reason Mind
- language
- interpretation
- meaning

Emotion Mind
- feelings
- sensations
- urges

Wise Mind

Behavior
Live in the moment,
and do what works!

The purpose of practicing mindfulness is to get in the moment and do what works. Mindfulness is different from meditation in that you can practice mindfulness at any moment in time and experience its benefits without having to close your eyes or sit or stand in any particular way. Developing a lifestyle of participation with awareness empowers you to gain access to your own intuitive inner wisdom to do what works in the moment.

What Skills

- **Observe.** Just notice your thoughts, feelings, behaviors, and whatever is going on inside and around you.

- **Describe.** Describe your thoughts just as they are, put words to your feelings, and describe your behaviors and experiences like a news reporter. Describe what you observe—no more, no less.

- **Participate.** Fully experience the moment without clinging to it or running away from it. If you are thinking of the past or future, just notice that and stay in the moment.

How Skills

- **One mindfully.** Focus on one thing at a time. Observe, describe, and participate with your thoughts, then your feelings, then your behaviors, and then your surroundings.

- **Nonjudgmentally.** Suspend your judgment of good, bad, right, or wrong, and do not make it mean anything. Avoid "shoulding" on yourself, others, and the world.

- **Effectively.** Ask yourself, "Knowing what I am thinking, feeling, doing, and what is going on around me, what will work best for me in this moment?" Do what works.

ACQUISITION

Creating a Life I Love: Study Guide
Session 2: Mindfulness

Reasons to Get in the Moment

There are many health benefits to practicing mindfulness. Consistent nonjudgmental awareness can reduce stress, boost immune functioning, reduce chronic pain, lower blood pressure, reduce the risk of heart disease, and make it easier to cope when you are sick. Being mindful makes you less critical and defensive and provides you easier access to self-esteem, love, happiness, and joy. It broadens the gap between stimulus and response and weakens impulses to engage in behaviors that interfere with creating a life you love.

We are creatures of habit. We simply think, feel, and behave in ways that seem to work for the moment and do it often enough that it becomes automatic. Think about what it is like to learn to walk, ride a bike, or drive a car. When you first began to learn something, your mind was very consciously focused on the new behavior. The more you repeated the behavior, the more natural it became, and the less aware you were of doing it. Even if habitual behavior stops working, it is difficult to change as long as we live on autopilot and without awareness.

You can create new habits. Mindfulness increases your awareness, takes you out of autopilot, and interrupts old, ineffective patterns. It provides a space so you can access your wisdom to create powerful and effective new ways of thinking, feeling, and behaving. Being mindful frees you from the restrictions of your past and the worries of your future.

Your past and future do not exist. They never have. Your memories are only interpretations of perceptions of what happened in your past, and your worries are only interpretations of perceptions of what might happen in the future. You cannot change your past or put it on a table for everyone to see because, like the dinosaurs, it is extinct. Of course, your future doesn't exist either. It simply hasn't transpired yet. It can be created only in the present.

Living in the past. When you live in the past, you cannot fully experience the present. You believe your way of being is fixed and unchangeable and compare what is happening in the moment with what happened in the past. There is a distinction between learning from the past and living in it. Possibility does not exist in the past. Habitually living in the past increases the probability that you will repeat it. If you don't want history to repeat itself, you must learn to put the past where it belongs—*in the past*—and let it go. The following are examples of living in the past:

- criticizing, blaming, or judging others who remind you of those who have hurt you in the past
- insisting that you have always been a certain way and that you will always be that way, even when your way of being continuously sabotages your health, relationships, career, or financial situation
- consistently comparing what is happening now with what happened in the past

Creating a Life I Love: Study Guide
Session 2: Mindfulness

Living in the future. When you live in the future, you cannot fully experience the present. What happens in the moment is a reaction to what you think might or should happen in the future. You are always preparing to live without ever actually living. There is a distinction between planning ahead and living in the future. Planning ahead and taking action in the present is much different from the inability to participate in the present without anxiety or fear about what might or should happen in the future. When you live in the future, the possibility that exists in the future cannot be realized. The following are examples of living in the future:

- persistently making plans, lists, and commitments to do something tomorrow or someday that never transpire
- being unable to experience moments of joy because of the anticipation of its end
- being paralyzed from taking action because of your fear of what might or might not happen

The present is all that exists. The present doesn't have a beginning or an end. It is the space and time with infinite possibilities where anything can happen. You can never choose to be or do anything in the past or future. Decisions and choices can be made only in the present, which is why being mindful of the present moment is so important.

Living in the present. To live in the present is to put your past where it belongs—in the past. It is to observe mindfully, describe nonjudgmentally, and participate fully in life from moment to moment without the constraints of the past or the self-fulfilling prophesies of the future. Every moment is a new reality. Along with living in the present comes the awareness that we never step in the same river twice. You see yourself, others, and the world with fresh eyes, experiencing the newness of each moment. Living in the present does not mean that you ignore the lessons of the past or fail to plan for the future. The present is the only place from which you can freely choose and act. Here are some examples of living in the present:

- focusing your attention on every bite of food, every sip of a drink, every step from one place to the next, every breath, every sensation and urge, and everything happening in and around you
- engaging in a conversation, sport, task, or hobby that captivates you so much that you lose track of time
- getting lost in a game, song, dance, or joke without worrying about what others are thinking or how you look

ACQUISITION

Practice Exercises

Being Mindful of the Moment

Become mindful of the moment and observe, describe, and participate with what is happening right now. Focus on one thing at a time without judgment and do what works.

What Skills

- **Observe.** Simply notice your thoughts, feelings, behaviors, and whatever is going on inside and around you.
- **Describe.** Describe your thoughts just as they are, put words to your feelings, and describe your behaviors and experience like a news reporter. Just describe what you observe—no more, no less.
- **Participate.** Fully experience the moment without clinging to it or running away from it. If you are thinking of the past or future, just notice that and stay in the moment.

How Skills

- **One mindfully.** Focus on one thing at a time. Observe, describe, and participate with your thoughts, then your feelings, then your behaviors, and then your surroundings.
- **Nonjudgmentally.** Suspend your judgment of good, bad, right, or wrong, and do not make it mean anything. Avoid "shoulding" on yourself, others, and the world.
- **Effectively.** Ask yourself, "Knowing what I am thinking, feeling, doing, and what is going on around me, what will work best for me in this moment?" Do what works.

Behavior: Describe what is happening or about to happen. Who is there? What are people saying or doing?

_____

_____

_____

Reason mind: Describe your thoughts, beliefs, interpretations, or assumptions.

_____

_____

_____

Emotion mind: Describe any feelings, sensations, or urges.

_____

_____

_____

Wise mind: Knowing what you are thinking, feeling, doing, and what is going on around you, what will work best for you in this moment?

_____

_____

_____

STRENGTHENING

Creating a Life I Love: Study Guide
Session 2: Mindfulness

Identify Interfering Behaviors

List three of your behaviors that interfere most with living a life you love.
Remember to write without judgment, criticism, or reason.

1. _____

   _____

2. _____

   _____

3. _____

   _____

Now choose one interfering behavior that you would like to replace, and complete the instructions below. You will use this to complete an interfering-behavior analysis in our next session.

1. **Interfering behavior:** Describe a behavior that interferes with living a life you love. Be as clear as possible, and describe it without judgment.

   _____
   _____
   _____

2. **Effect on life:** Check the areas of your life that are most affected by this behavior, and describe how each area is affected.

   ❑Finances ❑Education ❑Family ❑Health ❑Legal Matters ❑Occupation ❑Relationships ❑Social Life

   _____
   _____
   _____

3. **Setting:** Describe when and where your interfering behavior usually occurs. What is happening or about to happen? Who is there? What are people saying or doing?

   _____
   _____
   _____

4. **Frequency/Intensity:** How often does this behavior occur and with what intensity?
   _____ Times/ ❑Day ❑Week ❑Month ❑Year / ❑Weak ❑Moderate ❑Strong

STRENGTHENING

Home Fun

- Practice mindfulness throughout the day. Be mindful each time you change an activity, and be mindful of the many different activities you engage in.
- Be mindful of your interfering behaviors and those behaviors that work for you.
- Note what you were mindful of and the results of being mindful below.

_____

_____

_____

_____

_____

_____

_____

_____

_____

_____

_____

_____

_____

_____

_____

GENERALIZATION

Strategy: ## Interfering- and Created-Behavior Analyses

A behavior analysis is a strategy that mindfully examines specific behaviors in meticulous detail from beginning to end.

- An interfering-behavior analysis examines specific behaviors that interfere with creating and living a life you love.
- A created-behavior analysis helps you to create a desired way of being and choose matching behaviors that with practice become automatic and replace your interfering behaviors.

Purpose: Discover when, where, and how specific behaviors interfere with living a life you love. Create a way of being that inspires and moves you. Then develop a script to restructure your thoughts, regulate your emotions, and reinforce behaviors that match your created way of being. Practice and adjust your script until your desired behaviors become automatic.

Acquire: ### Training Topics

- learn from your past-interfering-behavior analysis: "It is what it is."
- create from your future-created-behavior analysis: "It can also be different."
- behavior rehearsals: "Practice, practice, practice."

It is what it is, and it can also be different.

Training Objectives

1. Identify triggers and rewards that move you to act on your interfering behavior.
2. Identify simple actions that if taken can reduce or eliminate your interfering behavior.
3. Discover what naturally motivates you. Understand that all behavior makes sense, you are doing the best you can, and nothing is wrong.
4. Create a way of being that inspires and moves you.
5. Develop a behavior-rehearsal script complete with thoughts, responses to emotions, and behaviors that match your created way of being.

Strengthen: ### Practice Exercises

- steps to complete an interfering-behavior analysis
- steps to complete a created-behavior analysis
- practicing and refining your created-behavior analysis

Generalize: ### Home Fun

- Complete an interfering-behavior analysis each time your interfering behavior occurs.
- Complete a created-behavior analysis.
- Practice and refine your created-behavior analysis at least three times each day.
- Note what worked.

ORIENTATION

Creating a Life I Love: Study Guide
Session 3: Interfering- and Created-Behavior Analyses

Learn, Create, and Practice

Learn from Your Past: Interfering-Behavior Analysis—"It Is What It Is"

Interfering behaviors are ones that you would rather not engage in but that continue to persist despite your best efforts to change them. An interfering-behavior analysis is a practical way of getting conscious or mindful of your thoughts, emotions, and behaviors that habitually occur in a specific setting and moment in time and interfere with loving your life. Your behavior becomes habitual when it is repeated often and the reward centers in your brain are stimulated during or immediately after the behavior. The effect is so powerful that an animal or human can be made to engage in a rewarded behavior so frequently that it will not stop to eat, even when deprived of food. The interfering-behavior analysis helps you to identify the triggers that set your interfering behavior in motion and the rewards that keep it going. This information will be used later in the created-behavior analysis to replace your interfering behaviors with new, desired behaviors. The interfering-behavior analysis is an acceptance strategy and is not intended to fix or change anything. It is important that you complete your interfering-behavior analysis mindfully—that is, simply observe, describe, and participate in the activity one step at a time without judgment. Once you have completed the interfering-behavior analysis, you can choose to accept your responses or create a new way of being and behaving.

Create from Your Future: Created-Behavior Analysis—"It Can Also Be Different"

A created-behavior analysis is a way of intentionally creating a desired way of being that inspires and moves you to restructure your thoughts, regulate your emotions, and reinforce behaviors that match the person you are creating yourself to be. It is then used as behavior-rehearsal script and practiced until the desired behaviors become automatic. Creating a way of being requires consistent commitment, repetition, reinforcement, and perseverance until it becomes as automatic as your interfering behavior is now.

Behavior Rehearsals—"Practice, Practice, Practice"

Because your interfering behaviors are already automatic and habitual, it is safe to say that they will occur again. The created-behavior analysis uses the same setting of your interfering behavior as a natural cue to practice your created way of being. There is no substitute for commitment, repetition, and perseverance when creating new behaviors. It is the same process you used when you learned to walk, ride a bike, or drive a car. You simply tried over and over again until you could do these actions without thinking. The same process is necessary to create new behaviors. Anticipate and welcome the setting where your interfering behavior occurs, and use it as an opportunity to practice the behaviors that match your created way of being. If you fall down, get up, and practice again. Remember: you cannot fail. You simply need to repeat the desired behavior enough for it to become habitual. It is also very helpful to practice your created way of being at times during the day when you are not as vulnerable to acting out your old ways. Like a professional athlete, you need to practice the basic strategies and skills you have learned every day and rehearse your created-behavior script until it becomes automatic.

ACQUISITION

Practice Exercises

Complete Your Behavior Analyses

Find the interfering- and created-behavior analyses forms in the back of this guide. You might want to make several copies so that you can keep the one in your book as a template. Complete an interfering-behavior analysis on a behavior that interferes with living a life you love.

Steps to Complete an Interfering-Behavior Analysis

1. **Interfering behavior.** Describe a behavior that interferes with living a life you love. Be as clear as possible, and describe it without judgment.

2. **Effect on life.** Determine the areas of your life that are most affected by this behavior, such as finances, education, family, health, legal matters, occupation, relationships, social life, and so on. Describe how each area is affected.

3. **Setting.** Describe when and where your interfering behavior usually occurs. What is happening or about to happen? Who is there? What are people saying or doing?

4. **Frequency/intensity.** Describe how often this behavior occurs and with what intensity. A behavior that occurs three times becomes a pattern. The strength of the pattern is determined by how often the behavior occurs. A pattern repeated daily is much stronger than one repeated yearly. The intensity of the pattern is determined by the strength of the urge to repeat it.

5. **Behavior.** Although behavior can refer to the behavior of your thoughts, emotions, or actions, this section refers specifically to what you perceive to have happened. Write what happened and what you and others said and did from beginning to end, one behavior at a time, in the behavior column.

6. **Thoughts.** Write the thoughts you were having when the behavior occurred next to each behavior in the thought column.

7. **motions.** Write the emotions you were experiencing when the behavior occurred next to each behavior in the emotion column. Score the intensity of each emotion with a number from 1 to 5, with 5 being the most intense, and write the number next to the emotion.

8. **Trigger.** Determine what you think triggered the event. A trigger can be anything that sets the patterned behavior in motion. A particular sense of sight, smell, taste, sound, or touch; a particular thought or emotion; or an event in the environment can all trigger thoughts and emotions that quickly generate a behavioral reaction. Determine if the behavior was automatic or acted on to get a certain consequence. Once you become mindful of your triggers, you can begin to have more control over them.

9. **Reward.** Based upon his extensive research, Dr. Steven Reiss proposes that there are sixteen basic desires or urges that drive much of your behavior. You can find the Reiss personality profile in his books *Who Am I? The 16 Basic Desires That Motivate Our Actions and Define Our*

Personalities and *The Normal Personality: A New Way of Thinking about People* (see Further Reading). According to his research, these desires are genetically encoded from birth and shaped throughout your life. Some desires are stronger and some are weaker than others. It is critical to understand that there is no right or wrong or good or bad desire. Identifying these desires helps you to understand why you behave the way you do. Knowing the desire behind the behavior lets you know that all behavior makes sense, that you are doing the best you can, and that nothing is wrong. With practice you can intentionally restructure your thoughts, regulate your emotions, and reinforce behaviors to intensely satisfy the natural desires of your heart and live a life you were born to love.

Review the sixteen desires listed on the interfering-behavior-analysis form. Use column A to check the desires you believe motivate you the most in your life. Remember there are no bad or good desires. Use column B to check the desires that are satisfied by your interfering behavior. Finally, use column C to check the desires that your interfering behavior keeps you from satisfying.

10. **Vulnerabilities.** You can avoid certain interfering behaviors simply by taking care of yourself when you are sick, taking time every day to do things you enjoy, maintaining a healthy diet, avoiding mood-altering chemicals, and getting enough sleep and exercise. The acronym PLEASE is designed to help you identify what you can do to be less vulnerable to acting out your interfering behavior.

11. **Result.** Determine how the incident ended. Why did you stop the behavior? What other problems were created?

12. **Intended solution.** What problem were you trying to solve? What did you want to happen? Was the solution effective for you and others?

13. **Pros and cons.** Identify the pros and cons of your behavior.

14. **Commitment.** Determine your commitment level (0 to 3, described earlier) to accept this behavior or create a new one.

In this training you will learn, strengthen, and begin to master effective, proven strategies and skills that will help you restructure your thoughts, regulate your emotions, and reinforce behaviors that will powerfully inspire and move you to create a life you love! However, you do not need to wait to create your desired way of being. If you have made a level 2 or 3 commitment, you are ready to take the next step. Complete a created-behavior analysis. Practice your script at least three times a day when you are least vulnerable to repeating old behaviors, and modify it until it works. Anticipate and welcome the setting where your interfering behaviors occur and take every opportunity to practice the behaviors that match your created way of being until they become automatic.

Steps to Complete a Created-Behavior Analysis

1. **Create yourself as a possibility.** Who you are is whoever you create yourself to be. Create who you are right now as a possibility and then restructure your thoughts, regulate your emotions, and reinforce behaviors that match your created way of being until they become automatic.

   a. Put your past where it belongs—in the past. It does not exist.

   b. Get in the moment right now.

   c. Create a way of being that inspires you, a way of being that moves, motivates, satisfies, and excites you to your very core.

   d. Choose your way of being as possibility rather than an expectation. Unrealized possibilities remain as possibilities. Unrealized expectations result in disappointment. You can decide to continue a way of being from your past or choose to create a way of being from endless possibilities that you have not yet experienced and seem completely unreasonable to yourself and others. Unreasonable does not mean impossible. It simply means your brain has no history to base it on.

   e. Complete the sentence "Right now I am the possibility of ..."

2. **Setting.** Describe when and where your interfering behavior usually occurs. What is happening or about to happen? Who is there? What are people saying or doing?

3. **Created-behavior script.** Fill out the reason mind, wise mind, and emotion mind columns as if the setting above is beginning to occur right now.

   - **Reason mind.** Describe empowering thoughts and assumptions that move you to act on your created way of being. *As a _____ person, right now I am thinking ...*

   - **Wise mind.** Knowing what you are thinking and feeling in this moment, describe what you are saying and doing to match your created way of being. *As a _____ person, right now I am saying and/or doing what works by ...*

   - **Emotion mind.** Use your wise mind to regulate your negative emotions and increase positive emotions. Describe the emotions that are elicited by your thoughts and behaviors. *As a _____ person, right now I am feeling ...*

4. **Behavior rehearsal.** A behavior rehearsal rarely takes longer than a few minutes. Practice at least three times a day when you are least vulnerable to act out old behaviors, and modify your script until it works. Be mindful of your vulnerable moments, and throw yourself into acting out your created way of being in that moment.

5. **Decrease your vulnerabilities.** Describe what you are doing to be less vulnerable to acting out your interfering behavior.

Practice and Refine Your Created-Behavior Analysis

1. Choose a time when you are least vulnerable to acting out your interfering behavior.

2. Use your mindfulness skills to get in the moment.

3. Imagine that the setting where your interfering behavior usually occurs is about to occur right now.

4. Say out loud, "Right now I am the possibility of …"

5. Read out loud what you are thinking, saying and doing, and feeling that match your created way of being right now.

6. Immediately reinforce your desired responses. Smile. Think or say something out loud to praise yourself. Do something with your body that moves you to feel excited, confident, and happy.

7. Rehearse and reinforce your created behaviors at least three times.

8. Modify as necessary to make the moment work for you, and practice again as if the event is occurring right now.

9. Remember that your current behavior patterns were repeated over and over until they became unconscious and automatic. There is no magic pill. Nothing can take the place of repeating and reinforcing new behaviors until they become unconscious and automatic.

10. Anticipate that because your interfering behavior has become a habit, the urge will occur again. The most powerful time to practice your new way of being is in the moment that your interfering behavior usually occurs.

11. Encourage yourself. Focus on your capabilities and strengths, let go of self-criticism, and genuinely assume that you are perfect, whole, and complete. Remember that you are doing the best you can, you cannot fail, and you need support.

STRENGTHENING

Home Fun

GENERALIZATION

- Complete an interfering-behavior analysis each time your interfering behavior occurs.
- Complete a created-behavior analysis.
- Practice and refine your created-behavior script as needed at least three times each day.
- Note what worked below.

_____

_____

_____

_____

_____

_____

_____

_____

_____

_____

_____

_____

_____

_____

_____

_____

Skill: # Restructure Thoughts

Your interpretations, assumptions, and styles of thinking have a huge influence over the emotions you experience and how you behave. As life happens around you, parts of your brain interpret sensory information into sight, sound, taste, touch, smell, and so on, while other parts interpret the experience to mean something based upon interpretations and meanings stored from past experiences. Although these stories of life are only interpretations, without awareness, you believe them to be true. Learning to separate your story from what happened frees you from the limitations of your past interpretations. It allows you to create any way of being you can imagine and to choose thoughts and assumptions that naturally move you to act on your creation. This training makes the assumption that we do not know the absolute truth. If a particular way of thinking does not work for you, try another way.

Purpose: Choose styles of thinking and empowering thoughts and assumptions that move you to act on your created way of being.

Acquire: ## Training Topics
- styles of thinking that may not work
- empowering constructs of thought
- how your brain processes traumatic experiences

Thoughts are nothing—no thing. It is from nothing that everything is created.

Training Objectives
1. Describe a style of thinking that may not work for you.
2. Identify thought constructs that work for you.
3. Describe what it means to let go of being right.
4. Describe what it means to replace expectation with possibility.
5. Continue to create yourself as a possibility, and restructure your thoughts to match your created way of being.

Strengthen: ## Practice Exercises
- letting go of being right
- replacing expectation with possibility
- letting go of stories that limit you
- practicing restructuring your thoughts

Generalize: ## Home Fun
- Practice letting go of being right with someone you have made wrong.
- Practice replacing your expectations of yourself and others with possibility and acceptance.
- Complete an interfering-behavior analysis each time your interfering behavior occurs.
- Practice and refine your created-behavior script using thought-restructuring strategies at least three times each day.
- Note the results.

ORIENTATION

Styles of Thinking That May Not Work

Researchers have identified some styles of thinking (listed below) that may seem to work in the moment but fall short when consistently and/or unconsciously used.

- **arbitrary inference**—drawing a negative conclusion not supported by the evidence
- **dichotomous thinking**—oversimplifying; interpreting every experience as black or white, good or bad, right or wrong, all or nothing
- **mind reading**—assuming one knows another's thoughts
- **magnification or minimization**—losing proportion; exaggerating or minimizing the importance of an event
- **overgeneralizing**—basing a general conclusion on limited data or just one incident; jumping to conclusions
- **personalization**—relating negative events to oneself without an empirical or rational basis
- **selective abstraction**—attending to only the negative aspects of a situation and ignoring the positive or neutral aspects; having a mental filter or selective attention; disqualifying the positive
- **creating catastrophe**—automatically assuming that the worst-case scenario will occur; telescoping of time and options
- **emotional reasoning**—having thoughts such as "Because I feel afraid, there must be danger"
- **overprediction**—believing the future will be repetitions of the past
- **overprescriptive**—insisting on how self, others, or the world should or must be

Empowering Constructs of Thought

Thought constructs. You were born into a world of thoughts. Thought constructs are ways of receiving, processing, storing, and using information. Interpretations, ideas, beliefs, and assumptions are merely constructs or symbols used to describe reality as we perceive it. From the moment you learned to use language to describe your experiences, your reason mind has been busy using thoughts to construct meanings about yourself, others, and the world around you. Your thoughts have a tremendous influence on your behaviors and emotions. Thoughts are constantly moving through your brain and, without awareness, can become automatic and fixed in a way that limits you from other possibilities. None of the thought constructs in this training are intended to be interpreted as true or right ways of thinking. If one way of thinking does not work for you, try another way.

What you know. Think about what you know to be true. Now think about everything that you know you don't know. Finally, consider the infinite amount of knowledge that you do not even know you don't know. Throughout history, humans have limited themselves because they were convinced they knew the truth. For example, people used to know the earth was flat, that witches caused the plague, and that you could never talk to someone on the other side of the earth or fly or go to the moon. Believing that you absolutely know the truth when you cannot possibly know what you don't know can create serious limitations in your life and keep you from experiencing possibilities you have not yet imagined. This training builds upon the assumption of the ancient Greek philosopher Socrates that we do not know the absolute truth. Another way to say this is "All I know is that I know nothing and that anything is possible!"

ACQUISITION

Creating a Life I Love: Study Guide
Session 4: Restructure Thoughts

Thoughts are not real. You cannot put your thoughts on a table and measure them. To demonstrate this idea, picture yourself in your mind. If you have a difficult time picturing things in your mind, draw a picture of yourself on a piece of paper. Next, imagine that your legs turn into car tires (or draw tires on top of your legs). Now imagine wings growing out of your back and you flying away. Now look at your real legs and turn them into tires or make wings grow out of your back and fly away. Notice that your thoughts can be changed in an instant, but no matter how hard you try, your legs will never turn into tires, and your back will never grow wings. This is because your legs and back are real and your thoughts are not. You do not have to act on your thoughts as if they are real. If a thought is not working for you, try another.

Your interpretations create your reality. What happened is what happened, and what is is what is; everything else is an interpretation. Consider that all you have ever been able to do is perceive your life experiences through your senses. Your brain interprets these sensations based on past experiences and makes them mean something. Because every life experience can have unlimited meanings, the ones you create are not really what happened but rather a story of what you perceive to have happened. This is why when several people witness an accident, each one has a different story. Your story about yourself, others, and the world is created somewhat like constructing a wall using bricks and mortar. Your interpretations of the experience (the bricks) are held together by your emotional reactions to the experience (the mortar). The more intense the emotional reaction, the more fixed in your brain the story becomes. Without awareness, your brain naturally collapses what happened with your interpretations of what happened and filters future experiences through the lens of this story. You then respond as if the story were true. This is not a problem if your story is a happy one. However, if your interpretations relentlessly trigger emotions of anger, anxiety, depression, fear, shame, guilt, disappointment, and hopelessness, then your story is closing you off to genuine experiences of self-esteem, love, happiness, peace, and joy.

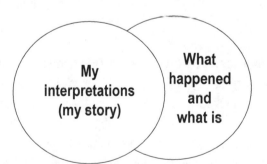

Separate your interpretations from what happened and what is. When you separate your story from what happened and what is, you discover that much of what you have believed to be true and unchangeable may in fact not be that way. Situations that may have been challenging or difficult become open to other possibilities. You find that you are no longer limited to a finite set of options and are now able to achieve what you want with new ease and enjoyment.

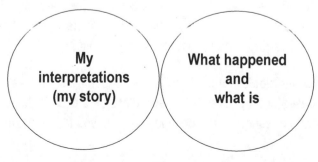

ACQUISITION

Meaning is what you make it. You will never find the meaning of life on top of a mountain, in the desert, buried in the earth, or in a book. This is because meaning is created in your brain. Your reason mind makes meaning of everything. In fact you may be reading this right now and asking yourself what all this means. Life itself has no meaning other than that which you create. You may have embraced someone else's meaning, and as soon as you do, they become yours.

Create meanings that work. The assumptions stated earlier—in fact, every word in this guide—is constructed thought designed to elicit emotions of self-esteem and love. These emotions move you to accept, improve, create, and give to yourself and others. If the meanings you have created work for you to live a life you love, keep them. If not, let them go, and create ones that do.

You are what you think. What you think can empower or weaken or inspire or discourage you. Your thoughts can be used to improve a situation, make it worse, or create a different situation altogether. Some people believe that our thoughts create everything. You usually believe your thoughts to be true even though they are merely perceptions. To paraphrase Henry Ford, if you think you can or are—or you think you can't or aren't—you're right. This reminds us of how influential our thoughts are to our behavior and general well-being. A more powerful way to state this thought is that you are who you create yourself to be. If you don't like who you currently are, create yourself to be someone you love.

> Choose your thoughts, for they become words.
> Choose your words, for they become actions.
> Choose your actions, for they become habits.
> Choose your habits, for they become character.
> Choose your character, for it becomes your destiny.
> —Author unknown

Your probable future. You experience life through your senses. Your brain then takes those sensory impulses and interprets them in ways that makes sense to you based upon similar past experiences. These interpretations are what make up your life story. After a while you begin to believe the interpretations to be true even if there is objective proof to the contrary. It is difficult to consider other interpretations because your brain wants to use the interpretations it has previously used and reinforced the most. If you are not open to other interpretations, your brain naturally triggers familiar cognitive, emotional, and behavioral responses even if they have proven to be ineffective. This may be one reason why you continue to make the same mistakes throughout your life. When you live your life based upon the interpretations your brain has stored since birth, you are living from your past. If this process is not interrupted, you can predict that your future will probably look very much like your past. In order to free yourself from this process you must accept that what you believe to be true is merely your brain's best attempt at making sense out of all the perceptions you have experienced since birth. You must then be open to consider and act upon possibilities that you have never considered or acted upon before. To do this you must learn to exercise your power to choose.

Choose versus decide. A decision is based upon reasons created from the memory of your past. A choice is based upon you choosing regardless of or even in the absence of reason. Making decisions based only upon your past understandings limits you to live inside the world of your interpretations and makes you a slave to your past. You do not have to be a slave to your past. You have the option to transcend your world of past reasons and interpretations and become whomever you choose to be simply because that is what you choose. Discovering the power of choice is like sitting in the corner of a cold, damp jail cell, feeling hopeless and defeated and resigned to never being free when you suddenly discover with great surprise and joy that you have been holding the key to the cell in your hand the whole time.

Be-do-have versus have-do-be. It is easy to get caught up in achieving goals and obtaining things only to find yourself becoming someone you are not really proud of. If you focus on your being first and then act on who you create yourself to be, when all is said and done, your goals and possessions will not define you, and you will have peace of mind in knowing you have been true to yourself.

Possibility versus expectation. Unrealized possibilities remain as possibilities. Unrealized expectations result in disappointment. Despite what your parents or teachers may have told you, you have never disappointed anyone, and no one has ever disappointed you. Disappointment is created by the person making expectations. You can avoid disappointment simply by replacing expectation with possibility.

Expectation	Possibility
⇩	⇔
Unrealized	Unrealized
⇩	⇔
Disappointment	Possibility

Create yourself as a possibility. Who you are is whoever you create yourself to be. You can decide to be the same person you have always been, or you can let go of your past and choose to create yourself as a possibility. Remember that if your possibility doesn't happen, it is still a possibility. Create a way of being that inspires you—a way of being that moves, motivates, satisfies, and excites you to your very core. Then restructure your thoughts, regulate your emotions, and reinforce behaviors until they match your created way of being.

Be unreasonable. If you create a way of being that has never existed before, your brain (and perhaps other people) will perceive your creation as unreasonable. Of course it's unreasonable! Unreasonable does not mean impossible—it simply means your brain has no past experience to base it on or reason with. Complete the sentence "Right now, I am the possibility of ..." Now align your thoughts, responses to emotions, and actions with your created way of being, and practice your new way of being until it becomes habitual and no longer unreasonable.

The glass is also half full. This course is not about trying to sell you on the concept of merely looking on the bright side of life. The glass is both half empty and half full. Both perspectives are valid, and when acted upon, each perspective generates its own consequences. This construct teaches us that whatever comes across our path in life, we have the choice to interpret it from a negative or positive perspective.

ACQUISITION

ACQUISITION

Let go of being right. Since all you have ever experienced is your perception of what happened, you cannot genuinely say that your way is the right way. Nevertheless, you often deceive yourself into believing that you are right. You pretend that your right is from sainthood and another person's right is from psychosis. There are certain benefits of being right:

- You get to be right and comfort yourself that others are wrong.
- You get to judge others and justify yourself.
- You get to dominate others before they can dominate you.
- You get to feel superior rather than inferior.

There is nothing wrong with being right. However, it all too often costs you love, joy, connectedness, and well-being.

Who we are. The following is an example of a personal thought construct. It is not true or false, right or wrong. It is merely a perspective that works for me.

Who We Are

We are human beings.
We are human; we are sensing, feeling, doing, and reason-making machines.
We are being; life being.
Our lives are empty and meaningless.
Life itself is empty and meaningless.
The idea that our lives and life itself is empty and meaningless
is itself empty and meaningless.
Our lives and life itself mean only
what we create each to mean.
We are nothing—no thing—
and out of no thing we can create anything or nothing.
Accept all things … change nothing … create anything …
the possibilities are endless!
Welcome to being …
who we are!
—Tim Bradley

How Your Brain Processes Traumatic Experiences

Your brain naturally processes and stores information received through your senses. Most experiences are processed immediately and others while you sleep. However, your brain does not always fully process experiences that have generated intense fear, anxiety, or sadness. These experiences are called traumatic. Most people have had experiences that have produced some level of trauma. Small traumas may result from experiencing painful physical injury or the unexpected loss of a loved thing, pet, or person. Big traumas may result from being emotionally, physically, or sexually abused; being responsible for the death of another; or having a personal near-death experience. The emotions and interpretations of traumatic experiences are so intense that your brain quickly locks them away in an unprocessed state. Unfortunately, because of the way your brain is structured, each time you experience a similar taste, touch, sound, smell, or sight, your trauma may be triggered, and you may reexperience the same fear, anxiety, or sadness that occurred during your traumatic experience. These unprocessed traumatic experiences can generate thoughts and emotions that can be so intrusive and debilitating that they have a negative effect on your self-esteem, personality, and relationships and cause serious dysfunction at home, school, work, and in the community.

The good news is that most traumas, big or small, can be fully processed. Eye movement desensitization and reprocessing (EMDR) and exposure are two evidence-based interventions that can significantly reduce or eliminate any trauma (see Further Reading). EMDR is provided by a trained clinician who helps you to get mindful of your trauma while utilizing methods such as eye movements and tapping that trigger your brain's natural processing mechanisms. Most traumas can be fully processed in three to four ninety-minute EMDR sessions. Exposure is a technique that also triggers your brain's natural processing mechanisms by intentionally and repeatedly reexperiencing or exposing yourself mindfully to the traumatic experience. It is critical that you develop appropriate mindfulness, stress tolerance, and emotion-regulation skills prior to exposing your trauma. It is also critical that you begin only when you are ready and stop yourself before becoming overwhelmed. Finally, you need to continue the exposure process until the traumatic story loses its power and you are able to report it as if it were yesterday's news.

Exposing yourself to your traumas can and will bring forth intense memories and emotions that can be retraumatizing and debilitating if not completed appropriately. If you have a history of severe emotional, physical, and/or sexual trauma, seek the assistance of a licensed mental health professional. If you do not have a history of severe emotional, physical, and/or sexual trauma, you can find an exposure exercise, "Letting Go of Stories That Limit You," in the following strengthening exercises section. You may want to wait until you have completed the rest of this training so that you have the appropriate skills to complete this exercise. Please do not take on this exercise unless you are committed to completing it in its entirety.

Practice Exercises

Letting Go of Being Right

1. Describe what you get upset about most often.

   _____
   _____

2. Describe how you behave when you get upset.

   _____
   _____

3. Describe who or what you are blaming, criticizing, judging, or interpreting.

   _____
   _____

4. Describe who or what you are avoiding being judged, blamed, criticized, or interpreted.

   _____
   _____

5. Describe how being right is affecting your life.
   A. What does it cost you? (love, peace, joy, etc.)

   _____
   _____

   B. What do you get out of it? (I get to be right, judge others, dominate others, etc.)

   _____
   _____

   C. Is it working for you?

   _____
   _____

6. Describe a way of being that works more with who you create yourself to be.

   _____
   _____

7. Let go of being right. Write a letter to a person whom you have had a consistent complaint about. Describe how you have tried to get them to be something other than who they are. Apologize for your judgment, criticism, dominating behaviors, and your superior attitude. Describe your new way of being toward them. You can keep the letter, discard it, or give it to the person you were making wrong.

   _____
   _____

Creating a Life I Love: Study Guide
Session 4: Restructure Thoughts

Replacing Expectation with Possibility

Expectation	Possibility
⬇	⬌
Unrealized	Unrealized
⬇	⬌
Disappointment	Possibility

1. Make a list of people or experiences that you have placed expectations on that were unrealized and that ended in your disappointment.
2. Describe how you thought they should or must be.
3. Radically accept that you and others are the way you are and the world is the way it is.
4. Create empowering possibilities of being for you, others, and the world.
5. Take responsibility for your disappointments, and apologize to those you have blamed for not meeting the expectations that you created.
6. Observe and note the results.

_____
_____
_____
_____
_____
_____
_____
_____
_____
_____
_____
_____
_____
_____
_____
_____
_____
_____
_____
_____
_____
_____

STRENGTHENING

Letting Go of Stories That Limit You

This exposure exercise is a powerful way of letting go of stories that are disempowering and limit your ability to live a life you love. Please be aware that engaging in this exercise can and will elicit intense memories and emotions that can be traumatizing and debilitating if not completed appropriately. If you have a history of severe emotional, physical, and/or sexual trauma, do not complete this exercise without the assistance of a licensed mental health professional. Even if you do not have a history of severe emotional, physical, and/or sexual trauma, you may want to wait until you have completed the rest of this training and have developed the appropriate skills to complete this exercise. Please do not take on this exercise unless you are committed to completing it in its entirety.

1. Set aside some quiet time, and write your life story from birth to present.
2. Take your time, and be as detailed as possible in describing what happened, what you were thinking, how you responded emotionally, and what you interpreted it all to mean.
3. After you have written your story, and only when you are ready, find someone that you know and trust who will just listen to your entire story without judging, criticizing, reacting emotionally, or trying to make it better.
4. Instruct your listener to simply listen to your story as you read it out loud without comment, emotion, or physical reaction. Read it as if you were reading to a computer. After you have finished reading, instruct them to simply say, "Again."
5. Do not start reading until you are ready, and stop whenever you think you need to.
6. Continue reading your story until you notice it losing its power over you.
7. It is critical that you not start this process until you are ready, that you stop when you need to, and that you complete the process until you notice the story has lost its power.
8. After completing this exercise you may want to destroy your story by burning it or tearing it up in a symbolic expression of putting your past in the past and letting it go.
9. Observe and describe the results of this exercise.

_____
_____
_____
_____
_____
_____
_____
_____
_____
_____
_____
_____
_____
_____

STRENGTHENING

Creating a Life I Love: Study Guide
Session 4: Restructure Thoughts

Practicing Restructuring Your Thoughts

1. Go back to your created-behavior analysis and restructure your thoughts, assumptions, and styles of thinking to match your created way of being.
2. Practice this new way of thinking in the context of your interfering behavior as if it is happening right now at least three times.
3. Observe any differences in behavior.
4. Change as necessary, and practice again at least three times.
5. Observe and note the results.

Home Fun

GENERALIZATION

- Practice letting go of being right with someone you have made wrong.
- Practice replacing your expectations of yourself and others with possibility and acceptance.
- Complete an interfering-behavior analysis each time your interfering behavior occurs.
- Practice and refine your created-behavior script using thought-restructuring strategies of your choice at least three times each day.
- Note the results below.

_____

_____

_____

_____

_____

_____

_____

_____

_____

_____

_____

_____

_____

_____

Skill: **Regulate Emotions**

How your emotional system works is quite complex. However, it is clear that how you feel has a great deal of influence over what you think and how you behave. The good news is that you do not have to be held hostage by your emotions. This session teaches you simple skills that can help you reduce your vulnerability to negative emotions or change them on demand and consistently create positive emotional states.

Purpose: Learn to recognize and regulate emotions so they do not regulate you. Decrease your vulnerability to negative emotions and increase positive emotions.

Acquire: **Training Topics**
- assumptions about emotions
- myths about emotions
- accepting your emotions
- decreasing your vulnerability to negative emotions
- transforming emotions through opposite action
- states of being
- creating positive states of being

Harness the energy of your emotions and you can be at peace, in love, and full of joy—even if you live in hell.

Training Objectives
1. List three assumptions and three myths about emotions.
2. Describe how to become mindful of your emotions.
3. List three practical steps to take to decrease your vulnerability to negative emotions.
4. Describe and demonstrate how to change emotions through opposite action.
5. Describe and demonstrate how to create positive states of being.

Strengthen: **Practice Exercises**
- becoming mindful of your emotions
- decreasing your vulnerability to emotions
- transforming emotions through opposite action
- increasing positive experiences
- creating positive emotional states
- practicing regulating your emotions

Generalize: **Home Fun**
- Be mindful of your positive and negative emotions throughout the day.
- Do one thing to reduce your vulnerability to negative emotions.
- Complete an interfering-behavior analysis each time your interfering behavior occurs.
- Practice and refine your created-behavior script using emotion-regulation skills and strategies at least three times each day.
- Note the results.

ORIENTATION

Creating a Life I Love: Study Guide
Session 5: Regulate Emotions

Assumptions about Emotions

- **Emotions are energies that move you.** Emotions move you to behave in predictable ways. They help you act quickly when necessary without having to think. The action urge connected to specific emotions is often hardwired.
- **Emotions can be triggered by your thoughts, behaviors, other emotions, physical or mental illness, food, drugs, lack of sleep or exercise, and your environment.** You do not have to be stuck in an emotion. Thinking and acting opposite to the emotion you are experiencing can generate an opposite emotion. Caring for your own physical and mental health can help you regulate your emotions and decrease your vulnerability to negative emotions.
- **Emotions have no meaning.** It is your reason mind that judges or gives meaning to an emotion. Emotions are not good or bad or right or wrong. They are just energy that moves you, like electricity running through a wire.
- **Emotions influence you and others.** Emotions communicate to and influence you and others, intentionally or not. Facial expressions are a hardwired part of emotions and communicate faster than words. Emotions can move you to give up, ruminate, fight, freeze, flee, hide, blame, or confess. They can also move you to improve, create, accept, sing, dance, smile, laugh, play, joke, give, and experience joy and love in your life.
- **Emotions come and go.** They are like waves in the sea. Most emotions last only a few seconds or minutes. Once an emotion starts, it can keep restarting itself. When an emotion seems to stay around, it is called a mood.
- **You are not your emotions.** Emotions are a biological response. You are no more your emotions than you are your heartbeat or body temperature. Just because you are experiencing an emotion doesn't mean you have to act on it.
- **Emotions can be regulated.** Unregulated emotions are like unpredictable, destructive weather and can cause serious problems in your life. Being able to skillfully regulate your emotions is like creating a beautiful, sunny day on demand, regardless of what the weather is like outside.

Myths about Emotions

- There is a right way to feel in every situation.
- Letting others know that I am feeling bad is weakness.
- Negative feelings are bad and destructive.
- Being emotional means being out of control.
- Emotions can just happen for no reason.
- Some emotions are really stupid.
- All painful emotions are a result of a bad attitude.
- If others don't approve of my feelings, I obviously shouldn't feel the way I do.
- Painful emotions are not really important and should be ignored.

ACQUISITION

Accepting Your Emotions

Be mindful of your emotions. Intentional focus on a specific emotion can reduce the intensity of the emotion or cause it to vanish altogether.

- **Observe your emotion.** Acknowledge its presence. Step back. Get unstuck from the emotion.

- **Describe your emotion.**

  - **Context.** When and where did the emotion occur? Who was present?
  - **Prompting event.** What started the emotion?
  - **Reason mind.** What beliefs, assumptions, and thoughts do I have of the situation?
  - **Body sensations.** What am I feeling in my body?
  - **Body language.** What were my facial expressions, posture, and gestures?
  - **Action urges.** What do I feel like doing? What do I want to say?
  - **Actions taken.** What did I actually do and/or say?
  - **Consequence.** What effects did my reactions to my emotions have on my mind, body, other emotions, and others?

- **Participate in your emotion by experiencing it as a wave that comes and goes.** Try not to block or suppress the emotion. Open yourself to the flow of the emotion, and experience it as it is. Do not try to get rid of the emotion or push it away. Do not try to keep the emotion around, hold on to it, or amplify it.

- **Focus on one emotion at a time.** Focus your mind on the emotion you are experiencing. If your focus starts to wander, observe the wandering and refocus. Notice that you may be experiencing a secondary emotion as a reaction to a primary emotion. For instance, you may be angry about being sad or ashamed of being afraid. Whether the emotion you are experiencing is primary or secondary, it is very difficult to maintain the presence and intensity of any emotion for longer than a few minutes when you intentionally focus on just that emotion.

- **Radically accept your emotion.** Do not judge your emotion as good, bad, right, or wrong. Acceptance does not mean that you agree or disagree, condone or condemn. Although you may not like how you are feeling, simply accept that your emotion is what it is. Remember you are not your emotion. Your emotion is simply an energy that moves you.

- **Do what works.** Does this emotion work for you? Is this emotion in alignment with who you are creating yourself to be? Do you want to change the intensity of this emotion or experience a different emotion altogether? Would avoiding nonprescription, mood-altering drugs; eating; sleeping; or exercising help to regulate this emotion?

Decreasing Your Vulnerability to Negative Emotions

PLEASE Build Mastery

Physical and mental health. Take care of your body. See a doctor when necessary, and take medication as prescribed.

Leisure activities. Develop a hobby. Do something you love to do every day, and get lost in it. Take time to stop and smell the roses. Notice when you are doing something pleasurable, and savor each moment. Cultivate an attitude of gratitude by regularly focusing on what you are grateful for.

Eat. Maintain a healthy diet. Stay away from foods that make you feel emotions that do not work for you.

Avoidance of drugs. Avoid drugs that make you feel out of control. Consume alcohol in moderation.

Sleep. Get at least six to nine hours of restful sleep each night.

Exercise. Check with your doctor to determine the amount and intensity of exercise that is right for you. Then schedule and engage in healthy exercise that works for you.

Build mastery. Do one thing a day that makes you feel competent, in control, and proud. Engage yourself in challenges that are just beyond your reach but can be attained using the skills you have learned. Then continue to learn and develop skills to master the next challenge.

ACQUISITION

Creating a Life I Love: Study Guide
Session 5: Regulate Emotions

Transforming Emotions through Opposite Action

Emotions are action-stimulating energies that are triggered by your thoughts, memories, behaviors, emotions, and your environment. They function to move you in a certain way.

Sometimes the emotions you experience do not work for the situation you are in. You may be afraid of the dark even when it's obvious there is nothing to fear. You may feel ashamed or guilty even when you have done nothing wrong. When your emotions do not work for you in a particular situation, an effective skill is to take opposite action.

Each emotion moves you in a very predictable way. By understanding how a particular emotion moves you, you can intentionally take the opposite action until the emotion of that action emerges. Your behaviors or actions communicate with your brain, and the effect is a slow but steady change in your emotions. Remember that facial expressions, posture, and body movement are critical to producing the desired emotion. For instance, if you intentionally smile, laugh, or dance, you will eventually begin to feel happy. Intentionally choosing thoughts, language, and actions that match the emotion you want to experience will eventually generate that emotion.

This is not to say that you attempt to bury or hide the emotion you feel originally. Being mindful of your emotion first helps you to get enough distance to act opposite of it. Acting opposite of your emotion works best if you throw your entire self into the process. It may feel strange and unnatural at first. However, the more you consciously and intentionally practice this skill, the more natural and automatic it will become.

The states-of-being chart on the next page is a brief list of common emotions and the thoughts and actions that elicit them. If a particular emotion is not working for you, find the emotion that you want to experience. Then think or speak the thoughts and act out the behaviors that match the emotion you want to experience until you feel it. Here are some examples:

- **Fear.** Fear moves you to fight, freeze, or flee. If you want out of fear, approach what you are afraid of. Do what you are afraid of doing rather than avoid it.
- **Shame.** Shame moves you to hide, justify, rationalize, or minimize. If you want out of shame, come out of hiding. Confess to yourself and others the effect of your actions. If there is no need to confess, simply accept your behavior as it is.
- **Guilt.** Guilt moves you to blame, judge, criticize, and eventually take responsibility, confess, and apologize. If you want out of guilt, take responsibility for your own thoughts, feelings, and actions, and accept yourself just the way you are, others the way they are, and the world just as it is.
- **Sadness or depression.** Sadness and depression move you to isolate, slow down, and stop. If you want out of sadness and depression, get out and get active. Do things that make you feel competent, confident, and pleased.
- **Anger.** Anger moves you to yell and fight. When you are angry, gently avoid the person you are angry with rather than attacking. Avoid thinking about him or her rather than ruminating. If you want out of anger, do something nice rather than mean. Accept the other person just as he or she is without making that person wrong.

ACQUISITION

States of Being

Thoughts, behaviors, and emotions combined for a period of time create your states of being. You can create any state of being by intentionally and consistently thinking and acting out the thoughts and behaviors of the desired state until the desired emotion emerges. The chart below describes a few basic states of being.

Emotion	Thoughts	Behaviors
Love	I accept you and me just the way we are and the world just the way it is without judgment. I do what works for you, me, and the world regardless of societal rules or laws and regardless of personal gain or loss.	Validate and accept self and others, give to self and others
Self-Esteem	I accept myself just the way I am without judgment. I do what works for my family, my friends, and me. As long as I'm not hurting anyone, it's okay. I have inalienable rights and personal beliefs that may supersede societal rules and laws.	Explore, improve, validate, and accept self
Guilt	I/you should have or could have been different or done something differently. I am, you are, or the world is wrong or right. Nobody is perfect. What about you? I obey rules because they are the rules and it is the right thing to do. Right must be rewarded, and wrong must be punished. Authority is not to be questioned.	Blame, judge, criticize, take responsibility, confess, apologize
Shame	I obey rules when the rule makers are watching. I want to look good and avoid looking bad. What people don't know won't hurt them. It's only bad if I get caught.	Hide, justify, rationalize, minimize
Greed	I must do whatever it takes to get what I want. If I want it, I get it. I should get what I want.	Earn, take
Fear	I must do whatever it takes to avoid punishment and/or pain.	Freeze, flee, fight
Anxiety	What have I done? What should I have done? What will I do? What should I do? What will happen?	Furrow your brow, pace, wring hands, shake a leg or foot
Sadness	I have lost what I love. I've been rejected or excluded. I am powerless or helpless to do anything about it. People don't like me. I'm no good. I cannot bear this. I would be better off dead.	Droop your eyes, face, and shoulders; move slowly or not at all; cry; isolate
Anger	I have been treated unfairly. I/they/it should be different. I'm right. They are wrong. It is wrong or unfair.	Clench your jaw and fists, snarl lip, hit, kick, throw, stomp, yell, curse, withdraw
Peace	What happened has happened. It is what it is. I am who I am, people are who they are, and the world is the way it is.	Relax your muscles, breathe slowly and deeply, accept
Happiness	Things couldn't be better! I love it. This is great!	Smile, laugh, play, joke, sing, dance

ACQUISITION

Creating a Life I Love: Study Guide
Session 5: Regulate Emotions

The Purpose and Effect of Positive States

Dr. Barbara Fredrickson (see Further Reading) has devoted her research to determining the effects that positive states have on people and how to increase one's positivity. Her broaden-and-build theory postulates that positive emotional states act to broaden a person's attention and cognitive awareness. The more frequently people experience and express positive emotional states, the more cognitive, behavioral, social, and physical resources become available to them, which, in time, increase positive emotions in an upward spiral.

The theoretical function of positive emotions is to broaden mind-sets and build resources. Positive emotions serve to build resources for survival by broadening the scope of awareness. This broadening of awareness allows a person access to a wider array of thoughts and action options. More thought and action options increase the probability of choosing more effective resources, which results in more positive outcomes. Positive outcomes tend to increase positive emotional experiences, which serve to broaden and build upon themselves in an upward spiral.

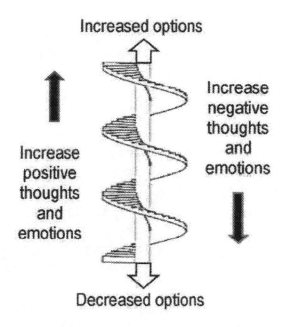

Take two minutes to complete the online Positivity Self-Test now at www.positivityratio.com. Your score provides a snapshot of how your emotions of the past day combine to create your positivity ratio. The higher your positivity ratio, the more resources are available to you and the more positivity you will experience. The good news is that you can increase your positivity through mindful and consistent daily practice.

Score yourself now and again every thirty days of using the skills in this study guide. Notice if your positivity scores increase. Especially notice how you feel about yourself, others, and the world. This test is an excellent barometer to determine how you are progressing at creating a life you love.

Creating Positive States of Being

- **Be mindful of positive experiences.**
  - Focus your attention on positive events in your life.
  - If your mind starts to wander to the negative, just observe the wandering and refocus on the positive.
  - Make a list of as many positive experiences that currently exist in your life as you can think of. Include those experiences that you have every day that you may not have been mindful of before.
  - Observe and describe your thoughts, language, behaviors, and emotions that are connected to your positive experiences.

- **Do pleasant things that are possible now.**
  - Do at least one thing each day that is positive and pleasant.
  - Focus your attention on all your senses.
  - Savor each moment.

- **Make changes in your life so that positive events will occur more often.**
  - Make a list of positive experiences you want to have.
  - List small steps toward goals.
  - Take the first step.

- **Build mastery.**
  - Do at least one thing each day that makes you feel competent, in control, and proud.
  - Engage yourself in challenges that are just beyond your reach but can be attained using the skills you have learned.
  - Continue to learn and develop skills to master the next challenge.

- **Replace your interfering behaviors with positive states of being.**
  - Choose the emotions you would like to experience in the same context that your interfering behavior normally occurs.
  - Create thoughts, language, and behaviors that naturally stimulate the emotions you are creating.
  - Practice your positive way of being at least three times a day as if the experience is about to occur.
  - Act out your positive way of being the next time you feel the urge to act out your interfering behavior.

- **Attend to relationships.**
  - Repair old relationships. Let go of being right. Remember that stories are just stories. Accept yourself and others just the way you and they are. Genuinely assume that you and others are perfect, whole, and complete; that nothing is wrong; and that everyone is doing the best they can.
  - Be open to new relationships.

ACQUISITION

Practice Exercises

Becoming Mindful of Your Emotions

Choose an emotion that doesn't work for you from your behavioral analysis. If the prompting event for the emotion you're working on is another emotion that occurred first (for example, feeling afraid prompted getting angry at yourself), then fill out a second homework sheet for that first emotion.

EMOTION NAME: _____ **INTENSITY (0–10):** _____

Context: When and where did the emotion occur? Who was present?

_____

Prompting Event: What started the emotion?

_____

Reason Mind: What beliefs, assumptions, and thoughts do I have of the situation?

_____

Body Sensations: What am I feeling and noticing in my body?

_____

Body Language: What were my facial expressions, posture, and gestures?

_____

Action Urges: What do I feel like doing? What do I want to say?

_____

Actions Taken: What did I actually do and/or say?

_____

Consequences: What effects did my reactions to my emotions have on my mind, body, other emotions, and others?

_____

Radically accept your emotion. Remember you are not your emotion. Accept your emotion as it is without judgment.

Do what works. If this emotion or your reaction to it works for you, then accept it as it is, and be at peace. If you would like to lessen the intensity of this emotion or change it altogether, accept the emotion as it is without judgment, and practice decreasing your vulnerability to emotions, taking opposite action, and creating positive states of being through the exercises in this book.

Decreasing Your Vulnerability to Negative Emotions

Identify which of the areas below may be contributing to making you more vulnerable to experiencing and/or reacting to negative emotions. Describe what you are doing in each of the following categories.

_____

_____

_____

Physical/Mental Health: Take care of your body. See a doctor when necessary, and take medication as prescribed.

_____

_____

_____

Leisure Activities: Develop a hobby. Do something you love to do every day. Reserve time to stop and smell the roses. Cultivate an attitude of gratitude.

_____

_____

_____

Eat: Maintain a healthy diet, and stay away from foods that make you feel overly emotional.

_____

_____

_____

Avoidance of Drugs: Avoid nonprescription drugs. Consume alcohol in moderation.

_____

_____

_____

Sleep: Get at least six to nine hours of restful sleep a night.

_____

_____

_____

Exercise: Check with your doctor to determine the amount and intensity of exercise that is right for you; then schedule and engage in healthy exercise each week that works for you.

_____

_____

_____

Build Mastery: Do one thing a day that makes you feel competent, in control, and proud.

_____

_____

_____

STRENGTHENING

Creating a Life I Love: Study Guide
Session 5: Regulate Emotions

Transforming Emotions through Opposite Action

- Identify negative emotions that you experience during your interfering behavior or at other times during your day.
- Write how the negative emotions move you to behave.
- Fill out the opposite actions for each negative emotion.
- Get mindful to the moment when you are experiencing the negative emotion as if it is happening right now.
- Imagine yourself taking opposite action to your negative emotion, and write the new emotion that emerges.
- Remember that emotions are just energies that move you. Your emotions do not mean anything, and you do not have to act on them just because you are experiencing them. You can transform any emotion you are experiencing.

Negative Emotion	Action	Opposite Action	New Emotion

Creating a Life I Love: Study Guide
Session 5: Regulate Emotions

Increasing Positive Experiences

- Focus your attention on positive events in your life. If your mind starts to wander to the negative, just observe the wandering and refocus on the positive.
- List up to five positive experiences that occur at different times in your life below.
- Include those experiences that you may not have been mindful of before.
- Next, make a list of positive experiences that you would like to create.

Daily positive experiences

1. _____
2. _____
3. _____
4. _____
5. _____

Weekly positive experiences

1. _____
2. _____
3. _____
4. _____
5. _____

Monthly positive experiences

1. _____
2. _____
3. _____
4. _____
5. _____

Yearly positive experiences

1. _____
2. _____
3. _____
4. _____
5. _____

Positive experiences I would like to create

1. _____
2. _____
3. _____
4. _____
5. _____

STRENGTHENING

Creating Positive Emotional States

Write the name of the emotion(s) that you want to experience and the thoughts and behaviors that stimulate the emotion for each context below, or create your own contexts that match your life throughout a normal day. Practice acting out each state several times until it begins to feel natural.

Context: Getting up in the morning

Emotions	Thoughts	Behaviors

Context: Going to work

Emotions	Thoughts	Behaviors

Context: When you are under stress

Emotions	Thoughts	Behaviors

Context: With your friends, partner, or child(ren)

Emotions	Thoughts	Behaviors

Context: Before going to bed

Emotions	Thoughts	Behaviors

STRENGTHENING

Creating a Life I Love: Study Guide
Session 5: Regulate Emotions

Practicing Regulating Your Emotions

1. Go back to your created behavior analysis and accept, regulate, or change your emotions to match your created way of being.
2. Practice this new way of responding to and creating emotions in the context of your interfering behavior as if it is happening right now at least three times.
3. Observe any differences in behavior.
4. Change as necessary, and practice again at least three times.
5. Observe and note the results.

_____
_____
_____
_____
_____
_____
_____
_____
_____
_____
_____
_____
_____
_____
_____
_____
_____
_____
_____
_____
_____

STRENGTHENING

Home Fun

- Be mindful of your positive and negative emotions throughout the day.
- Do one thing to decrease your vulnerability to negative emotions.
- Complete a behavior analysis each time your interfering behavior occurs.
- Practice and refine your created-behavior script using emotion-regulation skills and strategies at least three times each day.
- Note what worked below.

_____

_____

_____

_____

_____

_____

_____

_____

_____

_____

_____

_____

_____

GENERALIZATION

Skill:

Reinforce Behavior

Behavior refers to more than just your physical actions. For the purposes of this training, the word *behavior* refers to the way you think and feel, as well as your physical actions. Habits are simply behaviors that have been reinforced over and over again until they became automatic or unconscious responses. Your brain has been trained and is capable of being retrained to create new habits of thinking, feeling, and acting. However, your brain does not discriminate between interfering and effective behaviors unless you train it to. If you want to decrease or eliminate ineffective behaviors, you must consciously interrupt whatever is reinforcing them, replace them with more effective behaviors, and reinforce the behaviors that work for you until they become automatic. This process is most powerful when done in the moment the interfering behavior usually occurs, but it can also be effective if practiced as if it is about to occur.

Purpose: Learn how to use eight basic methods to effectively decrease or eliminate your interfering behavior and turn your desired way of being into habit.

Acquire: **Training Topics**
- steps to create new habits
- habit-making strategies

Harness the energy of your emotions and you can be at peace, in love, and full of joy—even if you live in hell.

Training Objectives
1. Describe the difference between respondent and operant behavior.
2. Develop and demonstrate your own way of immediately and positively reinforcing desired behavior.
3. Describe and demonstrate six reinforcement strategies.
4. Describe what naturally happens to your old behavior when you remove its reinforcers.
5. Describe why punishment is not effective in changing behavior.

Strengthen: **Practice Exercises**
- creating effective positive reinforcers
- practicing and reinforcing desired behavior while extinguishing interfering behavior

Generalize: **Home Fun**
- Complete an interfering-behavior analysis each time your interfering behavior occurs.
- Practice, refine, and reinforce your created behaviors at least three times each day using the skills and strategies you have learned so far.
- Note what worked.

ORIENTATION

Creating a Life I Love: Study Guide
Session 6: Reinforce Behavior

Steps to Create New Habits

1. **Become mindful of the forces that control your behavior.** Good intentions are often unrelated to actual consequences. In fact, many consequences are unintended. We may attribute certain reasons to why we do things when it is something unknown to us that actually stimulates the behavior. Completing an interfering-behavior analysis is a mindful way of discovering what actually controls your interfering behavior.

2. **Determine if your interfering behavior is respondent or operant.** Before you attempt to replace an interfering behavior, it is helpful to understand if it is triggered automatically (respondent behavior) or if it is rewarded by a consequence (operant behavior).
   - Respondent behavior is a behavior that occurs as an automatic response to a stimulus. For instance, if someone flushes a toilet while you are in the shower and the water becomes very hot and you jump back, over time, you will jump back automatically after hearing the toilet flush. A certain smell, sound, taste, a sense of touch, or even a certain look from someone can trigger an automatic reaction. Automatic reactions often lead to unintended consequences.
   - Operant behavior is strengthened and reinforced by getting a desired response as a consequence of the behavior. If you like people telling you how great you look and you go on a diet and people begin telling you how great you look, you are probably going to continue the diet so that you get more compliments.

3. **Commit to the process.** Creating new habits requires a level of commitment that is strong enough and maintained long enough to complete the process. Simply wanting to create something new is often not enough. Creating new habits can be compared to climbing a mountain or running a marathon. You must be able to see the end from the beginning and replace "I want to" with "Right now I am!"

4. **Create yourself as a possibility.** Create yourself as a possibility in a way that inspires, moves, motivates, and excites you to your very core. This provides you with the underlying mental framework from which desired thoughts, behaviors, and responses to emotions can naturally be attached and makes it easier to maintain the necessary level of commitment that is needed throughout the process.

5. **Replace and reinforce desired behaviors.** Choose a behavior or learn, practice, and generalize strategies or skills that align with the way of being you are creating. Then repeatedly practice and reinforce that behavior or skill in the same setting where the undesired behavior occurs. The term *reinforce* means to strengthen. Behavior repeats itself and becomes habitual when it is reinforced by stimulating reward centers in the brain immediately after or during the desired behavior. Completing, developing, and practicing your created-behavior analysis provides you with a clear vision of who you are and a practical way of replacing and reinforcing desired behaviors.

6. **Use reinforcement strategies that work.** The reinforcement strategies that follow are listed from most positive to most negative. There is no good, bad, right, or wrong reinforcement strategy. Experiment with different reinforcers and strategies and observe their effects. Mix and match reinforcement strategies and try different ways to stimulate your brain's pleasure center. If you find something that works, keep using it. If not, try something else.

7. **Keep at it until it's automatic.** There is no set number of repetitions required to create a habit. Remember that your current behavior patterns were repeated over and over until they became unconscious and automatic. The basic rule of thumb is to repeat the above steps consciously and consistently until the interfering behavior is replaced and the created behavior becomes unconscious and automatic.

Habit-Making Strategies

ACQUISITION

1. **Attend to your natural motivation.** You were born with a specific set of desires or motivators encoded in your DNA (desire to be accepted, desire for family or status or socialization or curiosity, etc.), and through the years those desires have been shaped by your life experiences. I highly recommend completing the Reiss Personality Profile from Dr. Reiss's book *Who Am I? The 16 Basic Desires That Motivate Our Actions and Define Our Personalities* or *The Normal Personality: A New Way of Thinking about People* (see Further Reading). Once you determine what naturally motivates you, then practice and reinforce thoughts, responses to emotions, and behaviors that result in attaining the natural desires of your heart in ways that work for you.

2. **Increase desired behavior with positive reinforcement.** Provide a rewarding stimulus during or immediately after the desired behavior occurs. Remember that your brain is a learning organism. When you reward yourself immediately following a desired behavior, the pleasure centers in your brain are stimulated, and your brain literally creates new neural pathways, which makes it easier to perform that behavior the next time. The more often you reinforce the behavior, the more automatic it becomes. As your desired behavior begins to occur more easily, you can provide a reinforcement every once in a while. This is called intermittent reinforcement and is a powerful way to strengthen behavior. If you have ever played in Vegas, you have seen how powerful intermittent reinforcement can be. You feed the machine money, push a button, and every once in a while, the machine pays you back. You may even get a jackpot. Intermittent reinforcement is so powerful that people will spend more money than they actually have. You may need to experiment with how you reward your desired behavior. It may be just by telling yourself, "Way to go," smiling, or giving yourself a treat. To be most effective, you must be able to give your chosen reward during or immediately after the desired behavior occurs. Create a reinforcer that incorporates your thoughts, emotions, and actions in a way that stimulates the pleasure center of your brain.
    *   Praise yourself in a way that elicits a positive emotion.
    *   Restate your created way of being. If you are not excited and inspired by it, change it until you are.
    *   Smile and do something with your body that elicits a positive emotion, such as snapping your fingers, clapping your hands, doing a little dance, or standing or sitting up straight.

3. **Put the interfering behavior on cue.** Choose a time to do the interfering behavior on purpose and on your command or cue. Often, consciously planning the undesired behavior is enough to interrupt its automatic nature and stop it from occurring. For example, couples who complain that their sex life has lost its zing are often asked to go home and intentionally avoid engaging in any sexual activity whatsoever. More often than not, they later sheepishly confess that they were unable to follow directions. Completing the interfering- and created-behavior analyses is another way of putting the unwanted behavior on cue.

4. **Replace and reinforce desired behaviors.** Choose a behavior or learn, practice, and generalize a strategy or skill that aligns with the way of being you are creating. Then practice and reinforce that behavior or skill repeatedly in the same setting where the undesired behavior occurs. Completing, developing, and practicing your created-behavior analysis is a way of replacing and reinforcing desired behaviors.

ACQUISITION

5. **Extinguish interfering behavior.** Extinction works by determining the reinforcers that are maintaining the interfering behavior and withholding them during and immediately following the behavior. Ignoring an interfering urge or behavior as if it does not exist is an example of the extinction strategy. Be forewarned, however, that if done correctly, the desire to act out the ignored behavior will at first increase in intensity. This is known as an extinction burst. If you continue to ignore the behavior as if it doesn't exist, the desire to act it out will eventually cease from lack of reinforcement, like a candle burning out from lack of oxygen. Also, because giving in to the urge or behavior once in a while (or intermittently) can actually make it stronger, it is more effective to use this strategy in conjunction with replacing and reinforcing the desired behavior.

6. **Negative reinforcement.** Negative reinforcement works by creating an unpleasant stimulus and keeping it present until the desired behavior occurs. A change in behavior must make the unpleasant stimulus go away. If the desired behavior occurs and the unpleasant stimulus does not stop, it is simply punishment and not as effective in creating change. The stress of having to complete a task may be a negative reinforcer if the stress goes away when the task is accomplished. Giving a child time-out is another example of a negative reinforcer, as long as the moment your child produces the desired behavior you set them free from the time-out. Completing an interfering-behavior analysis each time a major interfering behavior occurs is a form of negative reinforcement.

7. **Punishment.** Punishment occurs whenever you inflict some kind of pain or take something away prior to or immediately following a behavior. Most people unwittingly use punishment as a primary method to change behavior because that is all they have ever known. However, punishment does not change behavior. It merely suppresses it or forces it underground as long as the pain or threat of pain is present. Once the punishment is stopped, the behavior is likely to come right back. Another major problem with using punishment is that it focuses your attention more on the interfering behavior than the desired behavior. Consistent use of punishment can trigger a cycle of negative emotions such as fear, guilt, and shame. Use punishment with caution, and avoid this method as a primary way of changing behavior.

8. **Eliminate the source of the problem.** Sometimes the most effective way to avoid a problem behavior is to eliminate its source. This of course does nothing to change your behavior; it just takes you out of the environment that isn't working. It is an option after you have tried everything else or when you are convinced changing the behavior is just not going to work. Examples of elimination are firing someone, quitting a job, divorcing, ending a relationship, or moving away.

Practice Exercises

Creating New Habits

Create effective positive reinforcers. Create a reinforcer that incorporates your thoughts, emotions, and actions in a way that stimulates the pleasure center of your brain and can be done anywhere, anytime.

- Praise yourself in a way that elicits a positive emotion.
- Restate your created way of being. If you are not excited and inspired by it, change it until you are.
- Smile and do something with your body that elicits a positive emotion, such as snapping your fingers, clapping your hands, doing a little dance, or standing up straight.

Practice and reinforcing desired behavior while extinguishing interfering behavior.

1. Choose a time when you are least vulnerable to acting out your interfering behavior.
2. Use your mindfulness skills to get in the moment.
3. Go back to your interfering-behavior analysis and determine if your interfering behavior is respondent or operant. The interfering- and created-behavior analyses are designed to work for both kinds of behavior. Completing the interfering- and created-behavior analyses each time an interfering behavior occurs is a form of negative reinforcement.
4. Imagine that the setting where your interfering behaviors usually occur is about to occur right now. This is a form of putting your interfering behavior on cue.
5. Say out loud, "Right now I am the possibility of ..." This is a form of attending to your natural motivators.
6. Say out loud what you are thinking, saying, doing, and feeling that matches your created way of being. This is a form of replacing and reinforcing desired behaviors.
7. Immediately reinforce your desired responses. Smile. Think or say something out loud to praise yourself. Do something with your body that moves you to feel excited, confident, and happy. This is a form of positive reinforcement.
8. Rehearse and reinforce your created behaviors at least three times.
9. Modify as necessary to make the moment work for you, and practice again as if the event is occurring right now.
10. Remember that your current behavior patterns were repeated over and over until they became unconscious and automatic. There is no magic pill. Nothing can take the place of repeating and reinforcing new behaviors until they become unconscious and automatic.
11. Anticipate that because your interfering behavior has become a habit, the urge will occur again. The urge to act out your interfering behavior will probably become more intense. This is called an extinction burst. Ignoring the urge and acting out your replacement behavior is a form of extinction. The most powerful time to practice your new way of being is in the moment that your interfering behavior usually occurs. The more you ignore the old urges and reinforce new behaviors, the less intense the urge to act out the interfering behavior will become.
12. Encourage yourself. Focus on your capabilities and strengths, let go of self-criticism, and genuinely assume that you are perfect, whole, and complete. Remember that you are doing the best you can, you cannot fail, and you need support.

STRENGTHENING

Home Fun

- Complete an interfering-behavior analysis each time your interfering behavior occurs.
- Practice, refine, and reinforce your created behaviors at least three times each day using the skills and strategies you have learned so far.
- Note what worked below.

_____

_____

_____

_____

_____

_____

_____

_____

_____

_____

_____

_____

GENERALIZATION

Skill: # Radically Accept

There is nothing mystical about love. It is an emotion that like all emotions moves us to think and behave in certain ways. The core behaviors of love are validating, accepting, and giving. Validation is a respectful and loving way of responding to yourself and others just the way you and they are and the world just the way it is. It demonstrates the assumption that all thoughts, emotions, and behaviors make perfect sense in light of a person's genetic makeup, where and how they were raised, their past experiences, and their current environment. It is important to note that validating a person's thoughts, emotional responses, and behaviors does not imply that you agree or disagree with them or that you condone or condemn them. Validating yourself and others is simply a way of producing more love in your life.

Purpose: Learn the conversation of love that radically accepts yourself and others without judgment, balances the stress of change, encourages greater trust and openness, strengthens relationships, and moves you to live a life you love.

Acquire: **Training Topics**
- high and low facilitative responses
- validation skills
- dialectic responding

The amount of love in your life is directly proportional to the amount you accept, give, and create.

Training Objectives
1. Describe three purposes of validation.
2. Describe and demonstrate four low facilitative responses.
3. Describe and demonstrate four validation skills.
4. Describe how dialectic responding helps to resolve disagreements peacefully.
5. Describe and demonstrate the and-versus-but response.

Strengthen: **Practice Exercises**
- high and low facilitative responding
- validation skill practice
- dialectic responding

Generalize: **Home Fun**
- Validate at least one other person, and note the results.
- Practice dialectic responding using *and* instead of *but*.
- Continue to complete an interfering-behavior analysis each time your interfering behavior occurs.
- Practice, refine, and reinforce your created-behavior script at least three times each day.

ORIENTATION

Creating a Life I Love: Study Guide
Session 7: Radically Accept

High and Low Facilitative Responses

The way you verbally respond can facilitate intimacy, elicit emotions of self-esteem and love, and strengthen relationships. It can also facilitate resentment, signal others to avoid you, or push people away. The top four facilitative responses described below are more accepting, while the bottom four responses are more change-oriented. None of the responses listed can be classified as good or bad or right or wrong, and each may be effective at one time or another. To facilitate a loving and trusting relationship, use the top four responses and move to the bottom four responses only upon request. Although it is critical to examine your own interpretations of personal events, if someone else asks you to interpret their experience, focus on how that person interprets the event and validate his or her interpretation rather than providing your own interpretations. Give advice and use commands or directions sparingly. Avoid "shoulding" on yourself or others. Ask and validate what that person thinks is best to do in the situation, and command or direct him or her only if you have permission to do so and it works for the situation. The goal is to be aware of the effectiveness of the responses as you are using them.

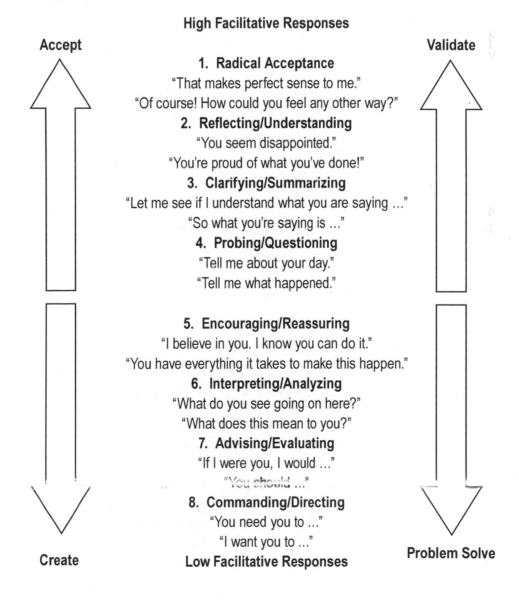

High Facilitative Responses

Accept / Validate

1. Radical Acceptance
"That makes perfect sense to me."
"Of course! How could you feel any other way?"

2. Reflecting/Understanding
"You seem disappointed."
"You're proud of what you've done!"

3. Clarifying/Summarizing
"Let me see if I understand what you are saying …"
"So what you're saying is …"

4. Probing/Questioning
"Tell me about your day."
"Tell me what happened."

5. Encouraging/Reassuring
"I believe in you. I know you can do it."
"You have everything it takes to make this happen."

6. Interpreting/Analyzing
"What do you see going on here?"
"What does this mean to you?"

7. Advising/Evaluating
"If I were you, I would …"
"You should …"

8. Commanding/Directing
"You need you to …"
"I want you to …"

Create / Problem Solve

Low Facilitative Responses

ACQUISITION

63

Validation Skills

Validation uses high facilitative responses to communicate radical acceptance and encouragement to yourself and others. It stimulates the emotions of love and self-esteem and creates more love in your life. Completing an interfering-behavior analysis of your own interfering behavior is a way of validating your own thoughts, feelings, and actions without judging them or trying to change them.

1. **Validate the story by asking open-ended questions.** We all have a story, and most of us love to have our story heard and accepted by someone without judgment, interpretation, or advice. Asking an open question such as "Tell me about your day?" or "Tell me what happened?" is really more of a request that gets someone to open up and tell his or her story.

2. **Validate the reason mind by clarifying what you heard.** As you listen to another's story, be mindful of the words he or she uses. Language is generated from your reason mind, and it is this part of the brain that invents the story. Accurately clarifying your own words and thoughts along with the words of another's story validates the reason mind. Think of clarifying as being an echo. The echo does not paraphrase or reconstruct a call. If you say "Helloooo" into a canyon, the echo doesn't ask if you meant to say something else or judge your call. It simply echoes back.

3. **Validate the emotion mind by empathizing with emotion.** Be mindful of your emotions or the emotions you sense from another person as he or she tells his or her story. Reflect them back as accurately as you can without judgment, advice, or interpretation. Acknowledging and feeling the emotions of another person is one of the most loving acts you can do. Think of yourself as a mirror. The mirror never looks back at you and criticizes or judges. It doesn't ask, "What were you thinking?" It just reflects what is in front of it.

4. **Validate the behavior and the whole person by communicating radical acceptance.** Create and communicate a genuine way of expressing radical acceptance such as "That makes sense," "Got it," or "Of course." This kind of acceptance is radical in that no matter what you hear or feel, you demonstrate complete acceptance for your own or the other's thoughts, feelings, and behaviors without criticism or judgment. Remember that validating yourself or another does not condone or condemn or make it right or wrong or good or bad. It's simply a way of demonstrating that all thoughts, emotions, and behaviors make perfect sense in the light of a person's genetic makeup, where and how that person was raised, his or her experiences, and his or her current environment. As simple as this skill may seem, many have not experienced this depth of acceptance.

5. **Encourage yourself and others by assuming the best.** Genuine encouragement intentionally sees the glass as half full and instills hope and inspiration to move forward in the face of fear or discouragement without giving up and throwing in the towel. When encouraging yourself and others, focus on capabilities and strengths, let go of criticism, and genuinely assume that you and others are perfect, whole, and complete and doing the best you can.

ACQUISITION

Dialectic Responding

Dialectics is a form of communicating that has been used to resolve disagreements and integrate opposing perspectives for thousands of years. Dialectic responding is based upon the principle that for any point of view, an equally valid opposite or complementary position can be held. For example, if someone is on a stairwell looking down at a group of people, he or she may describe what is present on the tops of their heads while others on the lower level may describe facial expressions. We wouldn't say that either observer has a wrong perspective. Both descriptions are valid from each one's point of view. Similarly, all individuals have their own unique perspective of life events that make perfect sense in light of their genetic makeup, where and how they were raised, and their experiences and current environment. Individual perspectives are not right or wrong. They simply are different ways of perceiving something. Dialectic responding moves people to be aware of alternate possibilities and encourages the integration of both perspectives into a peaceful and respectful solution.

Validate self and others: the and-versus-but response. Differences of opinion often result in an argument about who is right and who is wrong. Using *and* instead of *but* validates your opinion, as well as the opinions of others, without having to criticize or avoid criticism, dominate or avoid domination, or be right and make the other wrong. When your opinions and the opinions of others are presented as equally valid, it is easier to come to a synthesis of opinion or compromise that works for everyone involved.

For example, "It makes perfect sense that you (think, feel, do, etc.), *and* it also makes perfect sense that I (think, feel, do, etc.)."

Validate past and present. Another time to use this response is when others criticize you for who you are creating yourself to be by reminding you of your past way of being.

For example, "In the past, I (thought, felt, did, etc.), *and now* I (think, feel, do, etc.). That was then, and this is now."

Practice Exercises

High and Low Facilitative Responding

1. **Low facilitative responding.**
   a. Get a group of willing participants together, and then break into groups of three.
   b. Choose one person to be the facilitator, one to be the talker, and one to be the observer.
   c. When the instructor says to begin, the talker and facilitator will hold a conversation for about three minutes.
   d. The talker will discuss something he or she likes about himself or herself and something he or she would like to change.
   e. The facilitator must respond to the talker using only the four lowest facilitative responses.
   f. The observer will listen for each response and put a check next to the response each time it is used on the "Facilitator Report Card" that follows.
   g. When the time is up, the trainer will ask each person to rotate their roles until each has had the opportunity to be the talker, facilitator, and observer.
   h. At the end of the exercise, share your experiences with the group.
      - What thoughts, feelings, and urges did you experience in each role?
      - As the talker, what did you like or not like about speaking to the facilitator?
      - As the facilitator, what did you like or not like about listening to the talker?

2. **High facilitative responding.**
   a. Do the same as above and use the same topic.
   b. This time, the facilitator must respond to the talker using only the four highest facilitative responses.
   c. At the end of the exercise, share your experiences with the group.
      - What thoughts, feelings, and urges did you experience in each role?
      - As the talker, what did you like or not like about speaking to the facilitator?
      - As the facilitator, what did you like or not like about listening to the talker?

Facilitator Report Card		
Facilitator:		
Low Facilitative Responding	**Frequency of Use**	**Total**
1. Radical Acceptance		
2. Reflecting and Understanding		
3. Clarifying and Summarizing		
4. Probing and Questioning		
5. Encouraging and Reassuring		
6. Interpreting and Analyzing		
7. Advising and Evaluating		
8. Commanding and Directing		
Talker's response:		
Observer's response:		

Facilitator Report Card		
Facilitator:		
High Facilitative Responding	**Frequency of Use**	**Total**
1. Radical Acceptance		
2. Reflecting and Understanding		
3. Clarifying and Summarizing		
4. Probing and Questioning		
5. Encouraging and Reassuring		
6. Interpreting and Analyzing		
7. Advising and Evaluating		
8. Commanding and Directing		
Talker's response:		
Observer's response:		

STRENGTHENING

Validation Skills Practice

1. Pick a partner. Choose who will talk and who will listen and validate.
2. The talker will discuss something he or she likes about himself or herself and something he or she would like to change for about three minutes.
3. The listener will validate the talker using the validation skills outlined in this session.
4. When the time is up, the talker will score the listener's validation skills by checking each skill observed.
5. Switch roles so both partners have the opportunity to be the talker and the listener.
6. Share your experiences with the group.
   - What thoughts, feelings, and urges did you experience as the talker and the listener?
   - As the talker, what did you like or not like about speaking to the listener?
   - As the listener, what did you like or not like about validating the talker?

Validation Skills Report Card	
Validator:	✓
1. Validate the story by asking open-ended questions.	
Asked open-ended questions. "What happened? Tell me about it."	
Encouraged the story to be told step by step. "Then what happened?"	
Communicated and demonstrated acceptance of each part of the story.	
2. Validate the reason mind by clarifying what you heard.	
Elicited and reflected thoughts and assumptions accurately.	
Clarified thoughts without criticism or judgment.	
Communicated and demonstrated acceptance of the thoughts expressed.	
3. Validate the emotion mind by empathizing with the emotion.	
Provided opportunities for emotional expression.	
Clarified emotions without criticism or judgment.	
Communicated and demonstrated acceptance of the emotion expressed.	
4. Validate the behavior and the whole person by communicating radical acceptance.	
Elicited and reflected behaviors, events, and consequences accurately.	
Clarified behavior, events, and consequences without criticism or judgment.	
Communicated and demonstrated acceptance of the whole person.	
5. Encourage yourself and others by assuming the best.	
Assumed the best and utilized encouraging assumptions.	
Provided positive alternatives to criticism and judgment.	
Focused on capabilities and strengths.	
Talker's response:	
Listener's response:	

STRENGTHENING

Creating a Life I Love: Study Guide
Session 7: Radically Accept

Dialectic Responding

Validate Self and Other

1. Choose a partner.
2. Choose a topic about which you do not agree.
3. Take turns presenting your positions on the topic while validating the other and yourself using *and* instead of *but*.
4. Try to combine both perspectives in a manner that works for both of you.
5. Note the results.

"It makes perfect sense that you (think, feel, do, etc.), *and* it also makes perfect sense that I (think, feel, do, etc.)."

Validate Past and Present

1. One person will challenge the other's created way of being by reminding them of their past.
2. The other person will respond by validating the past and the present.
3. Switch roles and practice again.
4. Note the results.

"In the past, I (thought, felt, did, etc.), *and now* I (think, feel, do, etc.). That was then, and this is now."

Home Fun

GENERALIZATION

- Validate at least one other person, and note the results.
- Practice dialectic responding using *and* instead of *but*.
- Continue to complete an interfering-behavior analysis each time your interfering behavior occurs.
- Practice, refine, and reinforce your created-behavior script using the strategies and skills you have learned at least three times each day.
- Note the results below.

_____

_____

_____

_____

_____

_____

_____

_____

_____

_____

_____

_____

_____

Skill: **Respond to Stress**

Stress is mental, emotional, or physical strain caused by anxiety, pain, lack of sleep, or overwork. It may cause symptoms such as raised blood pressure or depression. Pain and stress are an inevitable part of life and, like the weather, cannot always be avoided or removed. Some say the only place to be truly stress-free is six feet underground. Emotional suffering results from not accepting and managing stress effectively. Swiss psychologist Carl Jung once said, "The more you resist, the more it persists." Learning and practicing skills that effectively respond to stress empowers you to let go of suffering and continue on your path of creating a life you love without becoming overwhelmed, making things worse, and giving up.

Purpose: Learn how to tolerate stress, stay in the moment without making it worse, and let go of emotional suffering.

Acquire: **Training Topics**

The amount of love in your life is directly proportional to the amount you accept, give, and create.

- activate your wise mind
- distract with wise mind (ACCEPTS)
- soothe your senses
- IMPROVE the moment
- explore the pros and cons of tolerating stress
- radical acceptance
- observe your breath
- half-smile

Training Objectives
1. Describe three distraction skills.
2. Describe three skills to improve the moment.
3. Describe and demonstrate radical acceptance.
4. Describe and demonstrate how to observe your breath.
5. Describe and demonstrate a half smile.

Strengthen: **Practice Exercises**
1. Complete the pros and cons for tolerating stress exercise, and commit to practice.
2. Review and practice each respond-to-stress skill.
3. Observe and describe the skills that work most effectively for you.

Generalize: **Home Fun**
- Practice responding effectively to stress.
- Continue to complete an interfering-behavior analysis each time your interfering behavior occurs.
- Practice, refine, and reinforce your created-behavior script while using the respond-to-stress skills and strategies at least three times each day.

ORIENTATION

Activate Your Wise Mind

- **Become mindful of your stress.** Observe, describe, and participate with your stress or pain without judging it as right or wrong, good or bad.

- **Accept your stress.** Accept that pain and stress are both natural and inevitable parts of life.

- **Do what works to respond effectively to stress.** The following coping skills are time-tested and empower you to let go of suffering and continue on your path of creating a life you love without becoming overwhelmed, making things worse, or giving up. They are not intended to be an exhaustive list. The first set of skills will help you effectively respond to stress through distraction, self-soothing, improving the moment, and exploring the pros and cons of tolerating stress. The second set of skills will help you practice radical acceptance.

Distract with Wise Mind (ACCEPTS)

Activities — Engage in activity, exercise, or hobbies; clean the house; go to an event; call or visit a friend; play a game; go for a walk; work; play sports; go out to eat; go to a movie; go fishing; chop wood; work in the garden.

Contribute — Contribute to someone or something; do volunteer work; give something to someone; make something nice for someone; do a surprising, thoughtful deed.

Compare — Compare yourself to others who are not coping as well as you; compare yourself to those less fortunate; watch soap operas; read about or watch coverage of disasters or others' suffering, and remember that things could be much worse.

Emotions — Do something that elicits different emotions; read books, stories, or old letters; watch TV, videos, or movies; listen to music or other recordings; do anything that elicits different emotions.

Push away — Mentally push the situation away; build an imaginary wall between yourself and the situation; push the situation away by blocking it in your mind; censor ruminating; refuse to think about the painful aspects of the situation; put the pain on a shelf; box it up and put it away for a while.

Thoughts — Focus your mind on different thoughts; count to ten; count colors in a painting, leaves on a tree, number of windows, and so on; work puzzles; watch TV; read.

Sensations — Hold ice in your hand; squeeze a rubber ball very hard; stand under a very hot or cold shower; listen to very loud music; have sex; snap a rubber band on your wrist.

ACQUISITION

Soothe Your Senses

Sight   Watch your favorite movie; look at nature; watch a sunset or sunrise; read your favorite book or magazine.

Sound   Listen to beautiful or soothing music or to invigorating and exciting music; pay attention to sounds of nature (waves, birds, rainfall, leaves rustling, etc.); sing your favorite song or hum a soothing tune; learn to play an instrument; call information numbers to hear a human voice; be mindful of any sounds that come your way, letting them go in one ear and out the other.

Smell   Use your favorite cologne or lotions or try them on in a store; spray fragrance in the air; light a scented candle; put lemon oil on your furniture; put potpourri in a bowl in your room; boil cinnamon; bake cookies, cake, or bread; smell roses; walk in a wooded area and mindfully breathe in the fresh smells of nature.

Taste   Eat your favorite meal; drink your favorite nonalcoholic drink; drink herbal tea or hot chocolate; treat yourself to a favorite dessert; put whipped cream on your coffee; sample flavors in an ice cream store; suck on a piece of peppermint candy; chew your favorite gum; get a little bit of a special food you don't usually spend money on (for example, fresh-squeezed orange juice); really taste the food you eat; mindfully eat one thing at a time and enjoy it.

Touch   Take a hot bath; put clean sheets on the bed; pet your dog or cat; get a massage; soak your feet; put lotion on your whole body; put a cold compress on your forehead; sink into a really comfortable chair in your home or find one in a luxurious hotel lobby; put on a silky blouse, dress, or scarf; wear your favorite clothes; try on fur-lined gloves or fur coats in a department store; brush your hair for a long time; hug someone; experience whatever you are touching; notice touch that is soothing.

ACQUISITION

IMPROVE The Moment

Imagery

Use your imagination to create a happy, peaceful, or relaxing place in your mind. Imagine the sights, sounds, smells, tastes, and touch in as vivid detail as possible. Go to this space in your mind whenever you begin to feel overwhelmed with stress. Imagine that you are using effective skills that help you create a life you love.

Meaning

Remember that nothing means anything until you make it so. Find or create some purpose, meaning, or value in whatever you are experiencing. Listen to or read about spiritual values that comfort you. Focus on whatever positive aspects of a painful situation you can find and repeat them in your mind. Make lemonade out of lemons.

Prayer

Open your heart to a supreme being, greater wisdom, God, or your own wise mind. Ask for strength to bear the pain in this moment. Turn things over to God or a higher being or let them go.

Relaxation

Relax your muscles by tensing and relaxing each large muscle group, starting with your hands and arms, going to the top of your head, and then working down. Listen to a relaxation tape. Exercise strenuously. Take a hot bath or sit in a hot tub. Massage your neck, scalp, calves, and feet. Breathe deeply. Half-smile. Change your facial expression.

One thing in the moment

Focus your entire attention on just what you are doing right now. Keep yourself in the very moment you are in. Put your mind in the present. Put the past where it belongs—in the past. Focus your entire attention on physical sensations that accompany physical tasks (such as walking, washing, doing dishes, and cleaning). Be aware of how your body moves during each task.

Vacation

Give yourself a brief vacation. Get in bed and pull the covers up over your head for twenty minutes. Rent a motel room at the beach or in the woods for a day or two. Drop your towels on the floor after you use them. Ask your partner to bring you coffee in bed or make you dinner (offer to reciprocate). Get a magazine or newspaper, and then get in bed with chocolates and read. Make yourself milk toast or other snack, and eat it slowly while bundled up in a chair. Take a blanket to the park, and sit on it for an entire afternoon. Unplug the phone for a day, or let your answering machine screen your calls. Take an hour break from hard work that must be done.

Encourage

Encourage yourself. Repeat the phrases "I can tolerate this," "It won't last forever," "I will make it out of this," "This too shall pass," "I am perfect, whole, and complete, and there is nothing wrong," and "I am doing the best I can."

ACQUISITION

Creating a Life I Love: Study Guide
Session 8: Respond to Stress

Pros and Cons for Tolerating Stress and Pain

Make a list of the pros and cons of tolerating and not tolerating stress and pain. Focus on your created way of being and your long-term goals. Remember times when the stress and pain have ended. Think of the positive consequences of tolerating stress and pain. Imagine how good you will feel if you don't act impulsively and you achieve your goals. Think of all the negative consequences of not tolerating your current pain and stress.

Tolerating the Stress and Pain

Pros	Cons

Not Tolerating the Stress and Pain

Pros	Cons

ACQUISITION

75

Radical Acceptance

Radical acceptance of pain and stress as a natural part of life frees you from increased and unnecessary suffering. It involves perceiving and accepting your environment, thoughts, emotions, behaviors, and the behaviors of others without making them wrong or putting demands on them to be different. It's like saying, "It's raining and cold, and that's the way it is. I cannot change the weather. I can complain about the weather, curse or condemn it, cry or yell at it, or I can learn to tolerate the rain and cold until it stops and gets warm. I might even be able to put on warmer clothes or go inside. Nevertheless, right now, it's rainy and cold, and that's just the way it is."

Observe Your Breath

Focusing on your breath is an excellent way to bring yourself into the present moment. This is not because the breath has some magical property but because it's always there with you and is an effective way of focusing your brain. Focusing your attention on your breath coming in and going out and breathing deeply and slowly are excellent ways to relax your body and relieve stress. Observe your breathing as a way to center yourself in your wise mind. Breathe in acceptance, and breathe out fighting with reality.

- Lie on your back, and breathe evenly and gently, focusing your attention on the movement of your stomach. As you begin to breathe in, allow your stomach to rise in order to bring air into the lower half of your lungs. If only your chest is rising, you are not using your diaphragm to fully breathe air into your lungs.

- Count your breaths. Breathe in counting to one, and then breathe out counting to one. Next, lengthen your by breath by increasing the count. Breathe in counting to two and out counting to two. Continue increasing the count and the length of your breath as long as is comfortable for you.

- Walk slowly and determine the length of your breathing in and out by the number of your footsteps. Practice increasing the number of steps with each breath.

Half-Smile

Smiling sends an automatic signal to your brain to release chemicals that improve your mood, help you relax, and reduce distress. Relax by letting go or by tensing and then relaxing your face, neck, and shoulder muscles. Next, half-smile with your lips slightly upturned and the outer corners of your eyes slightly creased. A half-smile often turns into a full smile. Practice half-smiling when you first wake, during free moments, while driving, when irritated, or whenever you are feeling stress. Half-smiling can be an excellent positive reinforcer.

ACQUISITION

Practice Exercises

1. Review your pros and cons for tolerating stress, and commit to practice.
2. Review and practice each respond-to-stress skill described previously.
3. Observe and describe the skills that work most effectively for you, noting those skills below.

_____

_____

_____

_____

_____

_____

_____

_____

_____

_____

_____

_____

_____

_____

_____

_____

STRENGTHENING

Home Fun

GENERALIZATION

- Practice responding effectively to stress throughout the week.
- Continue to complete an interfering-behavior analysis each time your interfering behavior occurs.
- Practice, refine, and reinforce your created-behavior script while using the respond-to-stress skills and strategies at least three times each day.
- Note the results.

_____

_____

_____

_____

_____

_____

_____

_____

_____

_____

_____

_____

_____

_____

_____

_____

_____

Conclusion

If you are among the courageous few who have actually completed this course and are successfully using the strategies and skills to create a life you love, congratulations! Remember that creating a life you love is not a single event but rather a moment-by-moment process throughout the rest of your life. The hope is that as you continue to intentionally create your life story you will be more mindful of what works in your life; that you validate yourself, others, and the world more often and without judgment; and that you are more equipped to restructure your thoughts, regulate your emotions, reinforce effective behaviors, and respond to stress in ways that work for you. After using the interfering- and created-behavior analyses for a while, you will find it easier to complete the process in your head without having to write everything down. I have found that I still use the forms on my most interfering habits. Remember that this system is not the right or only way to create a life you love. None of what you have read is right or wrong or true or false. If this works for you, that's great! If this or any other system doesn't work for you, try something else.

One of the most innovative and world-changing people of our time was Steve Jobs. Try to imagine what the world would look like without the iMac, iPhone, iPad, iTunes—you get the picture. Here is a quote from Mr. Jobs that I believe sums up the importance of this training:

> Your time is limited, so don't waste it living someone else's life. Don't be trapped by dogma, which is living with the results of other people's thinking. Don't let the noise of others' opinions drown out your own inner voice. And most important, have the courage to follow your heart and intuition.

Finally, our lives and life itself mean only what we create each to mean. We are nothing—no thing—and out of no thing, we can create anything or nothing. Accept all things, change nothing, create anything: the possibilities are endless!

Behavior Analyses

Interfering-Behavior Analysis
"It is what it is."

Name:_____   Date _____

1. **Interfering behavior:** Describe a behavior that interferes with living a life you love. Be as clear as possible, and describe it without judgment.

_____

_____

2. **Effect on life:** Check the areas of your life that are most affected by this behavior, and describe how each area is affected. ❑ Finances ❑ Education ❑ Family ❑ Health ❑ Legal Matters ❑ Occupation ❑ Relationships ❑ Social Life

_____

_____

3. **Setting:** Describe when and where your interfering behavior usually occurs. What is happening or about to happen? Who is there? What are people saying or doing?

_____

_____

4. **Frequency/intensity:** How often does this behavior occur and with what intensity?
   _____ Times/ ❑Day ❑Week ❑Month ❑Year / ❑Weak ❑Moderate ❑Strong

5. **Behavior:** Describe what you perceive to have happened and what you and others actually said and did from beginning to end, one behavior at a time, in the behavior column below.

6. **Thoughts:** Write the thoughts you were having next to each behavior in the reason mind column below.

7. **Emotions:** Write the emotions you were experiencing next to each behavior in the emotion column. Include feelings, urges, sensations, breathing, heart rate, and tightness in your body. Score the intensity of each emotion from 1 to 5, with 5 being the most intense, next to each emotion.

Reason Mind Thoughts, beliefs, interpretations, assumptions	Behavior What happened? When? Where? What was said and done?	Emotion Mind Feelings, urges, sensations, breathing, heart rate, muscle tightness

8. **Trigger:** Describe the thoughts, feelings, urges, sensations, and/or environment that you believe triggered this behavior.

_____

_____

9. **Reward:** Identify the desires satisfied by your interfering behavior.
   A. Check your strongest desires in column A.
   B. Check the desires that are satisfied by your interfering behavior in column B.
   C. Check the desires that your interfering behavior keeps you from satisfying in column C.

A	B	C		A	B	C	
❑	❑	❑	**Acceptance:** The desire to avoid criticism or rejection	❑	❑	❑	**Power:** The desire for influence of will
❑	❑	❑	**Curiosity:** The desire to learn	❑	❑	❑	**Romance:** The desire for sex
❑	❑	❑	**Eating:** The desire for food	❑	❑	❑	**Saving:** The desire to collect
❑	❑	❑	**Family:** The desire to raise one's own children	❑	❑	❑	**Social contact:** The desire for friendship
❑	❑	❑	**Honor:** The desire to behave morally	❑	❑	❑	**Status:** The desire for prestige
❑	❑	❑	**Idealism:** The desire for social justice	❑	❑	❑	**Tranquility:** The desire for inner peace
❑	❑	❑	**Independence:** The desire for self-reliance	❑	❑	❑	**Vengeance:** The desire to compete or get even
❑	❑	❑	**Order:** The desire for structure	❑	❑	❑	**Other:**
❑	❑	❑	**Physical activity:** The desire to move muscles	❑	❑	❑	**Other:**

10. **Vulnerabilities:** Check the area(s) below that are out of balance and make it easier for you to act out your interfering behavior.
    ❑ **Physical/mental health:** Are you feeling ill? Taking your medications? Are there symptoms or side effects?
    ❑ **Leisure:** Are you doing something every day that makes you happy? Challenges you?
    ❑ **Eating:** Are you eating too much or not enough? Healthily? Regularly?
    ❑ **Avoidance of mood-altering chemicals:** Are you using nonprescription, mood-altering chemicals?
    ❑ **Sleep:** Are you getting too much or not enough sleep?
    ❑ **Exercise:** Are you getting too much or not enough exercise?

11. **Result:** How did the incident end? Why did you stop the behavior? What problems were created?

12. **Intended solution:** What problem were you trying to solve? What did you want to happen? Was the solution effective for you and others? Yes ❑ No

13. **Pros and cons:** Note the pros and cons of your behavior.

Pros for Keeping the Behavior	Cons for Keeping the Behavior
Pros for Creating a New Behavior	**Cons for Creating a New Behavior**

14. **Commitment:** Determine your commitment level to accept this behavior or create a new one.
    ❑ Level 0—"I accept this behavior and will continue to do it."
    ❑ Level 1—"I want to create a new behavior but not enough to do anything about it."
    ❑ Level 2—"I am willing to work with a coach and be coachable to create a new behavior."
    ❑ Level 3—"I am in it to win it and will work with or without a coach to create a new behavior."

Interfering-Behavior Analysis
"It is what it is."

Name:_____   Date _____

1. **Create yourself as a possibility: Be → do → have.** Who you are is whoever you create yourself to be. Create who you are right now as a possibility rather than an expectation. Create a way of being that inspires, moves, motivates, and excites you to your very core. Then restructure your thoughts, regulate your emotions, and reinforce behaviors that match your created way of being until they become automatic. Copy and complete the sentence "Right now I am the possibility of ..."

_____

_____

_____

2. **Setting:** Describe when and where your interfering behavior usually occurs. What is happening or about to happen? Who is there? What are people saying or doing?

_____

_____

_____

3. **Created-behavior script:** Fill out the following columns as if the setting above is right now beginning to occur.

Reason Mind	Wise Mind	Emotion Mind
As a _____ person, right now I am thinking ...	As a _____ person, right now I am doing what works by ...	As a _____ person, right now I am feeling ...

4. **Behavior rehearsal:** A behavior rehearsal rarely takes longer than a few minutes. Practice at least three times a day when you are least vulnerable to act out old behaviors, and modify your script until it works. Be mindful of your vulnerable moments, and throw yourself into acting out your created way of being in that moment. Instructions follow for practicing and refining your created-behavior analysis.

Steps for Practicing and Refining Your
Created-Behavior Analysis

a. Choose a time when you are least vulnerable to acting out your interfering behavior.

b. Use your mindfulness skills to get in the moment.

c. Imagine that the setting where your interfering behavior usually occurs is about to occur right now.

d. Say out loud, "Right now I am the possibility of ..."

e. Say out loud what you are thinking, saying and doing, and feeling that matches your created way of being right now.

f. Immediately reinforce your desired responses. Smile. Think or say something out loud to praise yourself. Do something with your body that moves you to feel excited, confident, and happy.

g. Rehearse and reinforce your created behaviors at least three times.

h. Modify as necessary to make the moment work for you, and practice again as if the event is occurring right now.

i. Remember that your current behavior patterns were repeated over and over until they became unconscious and automatic. There is no magic pill. Nothing can take the place of repeating and reinforcing new behaviors until they become unconscious and automatic.

j. Anticipate that because your interfering behavior has become a habit, the urge will occur again. The most powerful time to practice your new way of being is in the moment that your interfering behavior usually occurs.

k. Encourage yourself. Focus on your capabilities and strengths, let go of self-criticism, and genuinely assume that you are perfect, whole, and complete, are doing the best you can, cannot fail, and need support.

5. **Decrease your vulnerabilities:** Describe what you are doing to be less vulnerable to acting out your interfering behavior.

- ❑ **Physical/mental health:** Are you feeling ill? Taking your medications? Are there symptoms or side effects?
- ❑ **Leisure:** Are you doing something every day that makes you happy? Challenges you?
- ❑ **Eating:** Are you eating too much or not enough? Healthily? Regularly?
- ❑ **Avoidance of mood altering chemicals:** Are you using nonprescription, mood-altering chemicals?
- ❑ **Sleep:** Are you getting too much or not enough sleep?
- ❑ **Exercise:** Are you getting too much or not enough exercise?

_____

_____

_____

_____

_____

_____

_____

_____

_____

_____

Further Reading

Dialectical Behavior Therapy

Bohus, M., B. Haaf, T. Simms, M. F. Limberger, C. Schmahl, C. Unckel, et al. "Effectiveness of Inpatient Dialectical Behavior Therapy for Borderline Personality Disorder: A Controlled Trial." *Behaviour Research and Therapy* 42, no. 5 (2004): 487–99.

Linehan, M. M. *Cognitive-Behavioral Treatment of Borderline Personality Disorder.* New York: Guilford, 1993.

———. *Skills Training Manual for Treating Borderline Personality Disorder.* New York: Guilford, 1993.

Linehan, M. M., D. A. Tutek, H. L. Heard, and H. E. Armstrong. "Interpersonal Outcome of Cognitive Behavioral Treatment for Chronically Suicidal Borderline Patients." *American Journal of Psychiatry* 151, no. 12 (1994): 1771–76.

Linehan, M. M., H. E. Armstrong, A. Suarez, D. Allmon, H. L. Heard. "Cognitive-Behavioral Treatment of Chronically Parasuicidal Borderline Patients." *Archives of General Psychiatry* 48, no. 12 (1991): 1060–64.

Linehan, M. M., H. L. Heard, and H. E. Armstrong. "Naturalistic Follow-Up of a Behavioral Treatment for Chronically Parasuicidal Borderline Patients." *Archives of General Psychiatry* 50, no. 12 (1993): 971–74.

Linehan, M. M., H. Schmidt III, L. A. Dimeff, J. C. Craft, J. Kanter, and K. A. Comtois. "Dialectical Behavior Therapy for Patients with Borderline Personality Disorder and Drug-Dependence." *American Journal on Addictions* 8 (1999): 279–92.

Linehan, M. M., L. A. Dimeff, S. K. Reynolds, K. A. Comtois, S. S. Welch, P. Heagerty, et al. "Dialectical Behavior Therapy versus Comprehensive Validation Therapy Plus 12-Step for the Treatment of Opioid Dependent Women Meeting Criteria for Borderline Personality Disorder." *Drug and Alcohol Dependence* 67, no. 1 (2002): 13–26.

Lynch, T. R., A. L. Chapman, M. Z. Rosenthal, J. R. Kuo, and M. M. Linehan. "Mechanisms of Change in Dialectical Behavior Therapy: Theoretical and Empirical Observations." *Journal of Clinical Psychology* 62, no. 4 (2006): 459–80.

Robins, C. J., and A. L. Chapman. "Dialectical Behavior Therapy: Current Status, Recent Developments, and Future Directions." *Journal of Personality Disorders* 18, no. 1 (2004): 73–89.

Safer, D. L., C. F. Telch, and W. S. Agras. "Dialectical Behavior Therapy for Bulimia Nervosa." *American Journal of Psychiatry* 158, no. 4 (2001): 632–34.

Telch, C. F., W. S. Agras, and M. M. Linehan. "Dialectical Behavior Therapy for Binge Eating Disorder." *Journal of Consulting and Clinical Psychology* 69, no. 6 (2001): 1061–65.

Turner, R. M. "Naturalistic Evaluation of Dialectical Behavior Therapy-Oriented Treatment for Borderline Personality Disorder." *Cognitive and Behavioral Practice* 7, no. 4 (2000): 413–19.

van den Bosch, L. M., R. Verheul, G. M. Schippers, and W. van den Brink. "Dialectical Behavior Therapy of Borderline Patients with and without Substance Use Problems: Implementation and Long-Term Effects." *Addictive Behaviors* 27, no. 6 (2002): 911–23.

Verheul, R., L. M. van den Bosch, M. W. Koeter, M. A. De Ridder, T. Stijnen, and W. van den Brink. "Dialectical Behaviour Therapy for Women with Borderline Personality Disorder: 12-Month, Randomised Clinical Trial in the Netherlands." *British Journal of Psychiatry* 182 (2003): 135–40.

Online Resources for Dialectical Behavior Therapy

DBT Self Help
  www.dbtselfhelp.com

Dialectical Behavior Therapy (DBT): Behavioral Tech LLC
  www.behavioraltech.org/resources/whatisdbt.cfm

Dialectical Behavior Therapy (DBT): Intervention Summary
  www.nrepp.samhsa.gov/ViewIntervention.aspx?id=36

EMDR Institute Inc.
  www.emdr.com

NAMI | Dialectical Behavior Therapy (DBT)
  www.nami.org › Inform Yourself › About Mental Illness

Narrative Therapy

Doan, R. E. "The King Is Dead: Long Live the King: Narrative Therapy and Practicing What We Preach." *Family Process* 37, no. 3 (1998): 379–85.

Etchison, M., and D. M. Kleist. "Review of Narrative Therapy: Research and Review." *Family Journal* 8, no. 1 (2000): 61–67.

Fish, V. "Post Structuralism in Family Therapy: Interrogating the Narrative/Conversational Mode." *Journal of Family Therapy* 19, no. 3 (1993): 221–32.

Madigan, S. "The Politics of Identity: Considering Community Discourse in the Externalizing of Internalized Problem Conversations." *Journal of Systemic Therapies* 15, no. 1 (1996): 47–62.

Minuchin, S. "Where Is the Family in Narrative Family Therapy?" *Journal of Marital and Family Therapy* 24, no. 4 (1998): 397–403.

White, M. *Maps of Narrative Practice.* New York: WW Norton, 2007.

White, M. *Narrative Practice and Exotic Lives: Resurrecting Diversity in Everyday Life.* Adelaide: Dulwich Centre Publications, 2005.

White, M, and D. Epston. *Narrative Means to Therapeutic Ends.* New York: WW Norton, 1990.

Winslade, John, and Gerald Monk. *Narrative Mediation: A New Approach to Conflict Resolution.* San Francisco: Jossey-Bass, 2000.

Online Resources for Narrative Therapy

The Narrative Therapy Centre
www.narrativetherapycentre.com/narrative.html

Learn What Narrative Therapy Is and How This Technique Can Help
www.goodtherapy.org/Narrative_Therapy.html

What is Narrative Therapy? Alice Morgan—Dulwich Centre
www.dulwichcentre.com.au/what-is-narrative-therapy.html

Positive Psychology

Argyle, Michael. *The Psychology of Happiness.* New York: Routledge, 2001.

Benard, Bonnie. *Resiliency: What We Have Learned.* San Francisco: West Ed, 2004.

Fredrickson, B. L. "The Role of Positive Emotions in Positive Psychology: The Broaden-and-Build Theory of Positive Emotions." *American Psychologist* 56, no. 3 (2001): 218–26.

Fredrickson, B. L. "Positive Emotions and Upward Spirals in Organizations." *Positive Organizational Scholarship.* San Francisco: Berrett-Koehler, 2003.

Fredrickson, B. L. "The Broaden-and-Build Theory of Positive Emotions." *Philosophical Transactions: Biological Sciences* 359, no. 1449 (2004): 1367–77.

Kahneman, Daniel, Ed Diener, and Norbert Schwarz. *Well-Being: The Foundations of Hedonic Psychology.* New York: Russell Sage Foundation Publications, 2003.

Kashdan, T.B. *Curious? Discover the Missing Ingredient to a Fulfilling Life.* New York: HarperCollins, 2009.

Keyes, Corey L. M., and J. Haidt, eds. *Flourishing: Positive Psychology and the Life Well-lived.* Washington, DC: American Psychological Association, 2003.

Kobau, R., M. E. P. Seligman, C. Peterson, E. Diener, M. M. Zack, D. Chapman, and W. Thompson. "Mental Health Promotion in Public Health: Perspectives and Strategies from Positive Psychology." *American Journal of Public Health* 101, no. 8 (2011): e1–e9.

Koeske, G. F., S. A. Kirk, R. D. Koeske, and M. B. Rauktis. "Measuring the Monday Blues: Validation of a Job Satisfaction Scale for the Human Services." *Social Work Research* 18, no. 1 (1994): 27–35.

McMahon, Darrin M. *Happiness: A History.* New York: Atlantic Monthly Press, 2006.

Peterson, Christopher. "Reclaiming Children and Youth." *Positive Psychology* 18, no. 2 (2002): 3–7.

Reiss, Steven. *Who Am I? The 16 Basic Desires That Motivate Our Actions and Define Our Personalities.* New York: Berkley Trade, 2002.

———. "Multifaceted Nature of Intrinsic Motivation: The Theory of 16 Basic Desires." *Review of General Psychology* 8, no. 3 *(2004)*: 179–93.

———. *The Normal Personality: A New Way of Thinking about People.* New York: Cambridge University Press, 2008.

Robbins, B. D. "What Is the Good Life? Positive Psychology and the Renaissance of Humanistic Psychology." *The Humanistic Psychologist* 36, no. 2 (2008): 96–112.

Seligman, Martin. *Learned Optimism: How to Change Your Mind and Your Life.* New York: Free Press, 1990.

Seligman, M. E. P. "Can Happiness Be Taught?" *Daedalus* 133, no. 2 (Spring 2004).

Seligman, M. E. P., and M. Csikszentmihalyi. "Positive Psychology: An Introduction." *American Psychologist* 55, no. 1 (2000): 5–14.

Snyder, C. R., and Shane J. Lopez. *Handbook of Positive Psychology.* New York: Oxford University Press, 2001.

Online Resources for Positive Psychology

Action for Happiness
   www.actionforhappiness.org

Martin Seligman—Positive Psychology
   www.pursuit-of-happiness.org

Positive Psychology Center
   www.ppc.sas.upenn.edu

PositivityRatio.com—Self-Test
   www.positivityratio.com/single.php

Sample, I. "How to Be Happy," *Guardian UK*, May 18, 2010, http://www.guardian.co.uk/society/2003/nov/19/1.

About the Book

Creating a Life I Love: Study Guide removes the mysticism and psychobabble that often accompany the therapeutic and life-coaching process and systematically presents practical strategies and skills validated through research to effectively replace unwanted habits with desirable ones. Many of the strategies and skills presented in this study guide have been adapted from dialectical behavior therapy (DBT) developed by psychologist Dr. Marsha Linehan. DBT is currently one of the most effective treatments for depression, anxiety, suicide prevention, eating disorders, and substance abuse. The major premise of this book is that the same strategies and skills used to decrease patient dysfunction can also be used to empower mentally healthy people to significantly increase their own self-esteem, joy, positivity, and capacity to love.

The author postulates that the *human* part of human being is comprised of three distinct interconnected systems that produce thoughts, emotions, and behaviors. Each system has a specific way of functioning that is predictably mechanical and, once understood, easy to manipulate. The *being* part of human being is what the author refers to as the "I am." It is the part that observes, describes, and creates without judgment. It is the "I am" that possesses the executive power to override thoughts, emotional responses, and behaviors that do not work and replace them with ones that do. *Creating a Life I Love* was designed for any person seriously committed to self-help and personal growth. It represents a partial fulfillment to the author's lifelong dream of providing people in all walks of life with simple and effective tools that stimulate a radical and profound sense of peace, joy, and love for self, others, and the world.

About the Author

Tim and his family live in Southern California. He is happily married to his best friend and wife, Lynne, and is the proud father to two adult daughters, Kristin and Kelsey. Tim has been a licensed marriage and family therapist in the state of California since 1994 and a clinical supervisor since 2001. He has provided individual and group mental and behavioral health services to at-risk children, adolescents, adults, and special-needs consumers in school-based, residential, outpatient, and inpatient settings. Tim has received advanced training in dialectical behavior therapy through Dr. Marsha Linehan and her team and has been a master trainer and provider of dialectical behavior therapy to both consumers and mental health providers for over a decade. He is the founder and CEO of PathWise Productions Inc., a consultation and training company serving hundreds of psychologists, nurses, and mental health providers in Southern California. He is the author of six training manuals designed to increase consumer skills, employee skills, productivity, and job satisfaction. Tim is passionate about discovering and using the most effective, evidence-based methods available to help ease people's suffering and support their personal growth.

Contact Information:

Tim Bradley, MA, LMFT
PathWise Productions Inc.
Phone: 909-921-6466
E-Mail: tim@pathwiseproductions.com or visit pathwiseproductions.com for more information.

Printed in the United States
By Bookmasters